The Queen of Education

LouAnne Johnson

The Queen of Education

Rules for Making School Work

JOSSEY-BASS
A Wiley Imprint
www.josseybass.com

Published by Jossey-Bass
A Wiley Imprint
989 Market Street, San Francisco, CA 94103-1741   www.josseybass.com

Jossey-Bass books and products are available through most bookstores. To contact Jossey-Bass
directly call our Customer Care Department within the U.S. at 800-956-7739, outside the
U.S. at 317-572-3986, or fax 317-572-4002.

Jossey-Bass also publishes its books in a variety of electronic formats. Some content that
appears in print may not be available in electronic books.

Readers should be aware that Internet Websites listed in this work may have changed or
disappeared between when this work was written and when it is read.

Library of Congress Cataloging-in-Publication Data
Johnson, LouAnne.
  The Queen of education : rules for making school work /
LouAnne Johnson.— 1st ed.
     p. cm. — (The Jossey-Bass education series)
  Includes index.
  ISBN 0-7879-7470-6 (alk. paper)
1. School improvement programs—United States.
2. Education—United States—Philosophy. I. Title. II. Series.
  LB2822.82.J66 2004
  371.2—dc22   2004004031

Printed in the United States of America
FIRST EDITION
HB Printing   10 9 8 7 6 5 4 3 2 1

The Jossey-Bass Education Series

Contents

Introduction   xi

Acknowledgments   xv

The Author   xvii

Prologue: The Richest Country in the World—
A Twenty-First-Century Fable   1

1.   The Queen of Education   15

2.   Questions That Keep Me Awake at Night   25

3.   The Accidental Teacher   33

4.   Memo to the Boss   51

5.   Down with Detention   65

6.   Dear Miss J   81

7.   Truth in Labeling   95

8.   Hey Miss J!   111

9.   Scotopic Sensitivity   129

10.   The Big Fat Problem   143

11.   Why I Wouldn't Give My Own Kid Ritalin   153

12.   My Dream School   171

Epilogue: An Open Letter to Teachers   193

Appendix: Two-Minute Reviews   195

Index   213

Introduction

I used to find it amusing when reporters would check the clock, thrust their microphones in my face, and say, "We have thirty seconds left. What do we need to do to fix our schools?"

The first few times that happened, I spent the thirty seconds trying to decide which of a hundred things should be done first. Eventually, I hit upon the perfect answer: "Fixing our schools will take a lot of work, but make me queen of education and I'll see that the job gets done."

I admit I was being facetious. But after volunteering several times for the nonexistent job, I realized that this country does need a queen of education. We need a person who can take action: who can cut the ribbons of red tape, deflate the bureaucratic bloat, dismantle the diagnostic nightmare of attention deficit hyperactivity disorder, and stop the selling of our children to the highest corporate bidders. We need somebody who has common sense, somebody who puts children first and politics last. This book is my bid for the royal position. I'm not the best teacher in the world. But I am a very good teacher, and I do care passionately about improving public education.

Our schools are badly broken, but I believe they are still fixable. The fixing will require money, of course, but all the money in the world won't help if we don't change our fundamental approach. In my opinion the primary focus of our public schools today is not on educating children; the focus is on ease of administering schools. Obviously, it is cheaper and easier to group children by age, divide them evenly among classrooms, demand that they all progress at the same rate, and punish them when they revolt against a system that ignores their humanity.

We cannot mandate success in our schools. Testing teachers and students may result in higher scores on a specific test, but testing won't solve the problems—because it isn't the teachers and students who are broken.

We know what we need to do. Time and again small public schools, private schools, charter schools, schools within schools, alternative schools, mentor programs, school-to-work programs, and homeschooling programs have demonstrated that when we focus on students instead of administration, students succeed, even students who have consistently failed. Administrators themselves are not the source of the problem. Many administrators do place children first, but they struggle every day against overwhelming obstacles inherent in a system that is careening toward self-destruction with frightening speed, leaving a heartbreaking trail of illiteracy in its wake.

We could fix our public schools if we honestly embraced the philosophy of those successful small schools: a belief that all children can learn, that different learning styles must be accommodated, that some so-called "learning disabilities" are due to emotional instability or inadequate lighting or nutritional deficiencies, and that all children deserve to be treated with dignity and respect. But instead of adopting the approach of those small schools, we replicate the logistics and administration of those successful programs. We duplicate their facilities and curriculum and assessment methods. We consolidate several small schools (where students receive the personal attention they need) into huge impersonal conglomerates that reduce children to anonymous numbers. And then we go right back to focusing on administration instead of education. We ignore the most important piece of the puzzle and then wonder why we can't make the picture come out right.

I am the product of public schools, where I met teachers who literally shaped my life by planting the seed and nurturing the dream that blossomed into my career as a professional writer. After nine years as a journalist on active military duty, I decided to pursue a different dream: doing my part to improve our public schools and passing on the gifts of love and hope that my public school teachers gave to me. Fortunately, I was assigned to teach a class of "unteachable" students who appreciated those gifts and repaid me by succeeding in spite of the poverty, abuse, and violence that threatened to turn them into teenage statistics. Those students inspired me to tell their story in *My Posse Don't Do Homework*, which was later adapted for the movie *Dangerous Minds*.

Since *My Posse Don't Do Homework* was first published in 1992, parents, teachers, and students from all over the world have sent me letters and e-mail messages in which they shared their stories, their frustrations, their successes, and their dreams.(As always, I have changed students' names to protect their dignity and privacy.) This book is for those students and parents and teachers, for the people who still believe we can and should save our public schools

Acknowledgments

Special thanks to my teachers and colleagues: Mary Ellen Boyling, Kathy Chappel, Michael Colin, Ed Dickey, Nancy Eisenstein, Joann Fallon, Krystal Hall, Evelyn Hodak, Fiona Kellet, Monica Khoury, Courtney Madden, Ron McNeel, Michael Morehead, Joan Neller, Wayne Peterson, Eleanora Sandblade, Fred Stoller, Peter Thompson, Shellie Todd, Tawana Washington, and Liz Whitehead.

My gratitude to Alfredo Santana and Lesley Iura for editorial advice, moral support, inspiration, and occasional hand-holding during the writing of this book.

A huge hug for my former students, especially the ones who have written recently to let me know that they still remember me fondly even though I sometimes made them write two whole pages in their journals: Elias Alberda, Chris Cahill, Jenny Gramkan, Brandon Green, Alex Gonzalez, Oscar Guerra, Jessi Harrison, Ivan Hernandez, Robert Higareda, Nikki Bergquist Iffla, Jose M. Jimenez, Shaun Klansnic, Maria del Carmen Miranda, Dan Mueller, Juan Ortiz, Danny Robertson, Gennie Simms, and Ryan Wageman.

And as always, a kiss to my mother, Shirley Alyce Lauffenberger Johnson, who I believe is keeping an eye on me from her perch in the heavenly clouds above my house.

The Author

LouAnne Johnson is a former U.S. Navy journalist, U.S. Marine Corps officer, high school teacher, college instructor, and the author of the *New York Times* best-seller *Dangerous Minds* (originally titled *My Posse Don't Do Homework*). She is now a private tutor, author, student advocate, and educational consultant.

Born in rural northwestern Pennsylvania, Johnson enlisted in the U.S. Navy in 1971 and served eight years on active duty, achieving the rank of petty officer first class. She was awarded the Navy Commendation Medal and the Air Force Achievement Award for her work as a journalist and radio and television broadcaster. She earned a B.S. in psychology while on active duty, then completed U.S. Marine Corps Officer Candidate School, where she earned the title of honor woman, 116th Women Officer Candidate Company, and was commissioned a second lieutenant.

Following her honorable discharge from military service, Johnson returned to college and earned a secondary teaching credential and a master's degree in teaching English. Between 1989 and 1993, Johnson taught English at a high school in San Mateo County, California, where she also served as part of the teaching team for a Computer Academy school within a school program for at-risk teens. During her second year on the Academy team, Johnson was appointed department chair for the Academy. During the government evaluation of the ten pilot programs, Johnson's group was rated first in higher grade point averages, increased self-esteem, academic achievement, and student retention.

In 1993, Johnson moved to New Mexico, where she taught English and literature at a number of high schools and colleges for eight years before deciding to devote her time to improving our public schools through writing, consulting, and teacher training.

Johnson is the author of five nonfiction books: *Making Waves: A Woman in This Man's Navy* (St. Martin's Press, 1986); *My Posse Don't Do Homework* (St. Martin's Press, 1992), republished as *Dangerous Minds* (St. Martin's Press, 1995); *The Girls in the Back of the Class* (St. Martin's Press, 1995); *School Is Not a Four-Letter Word* (Hyperion, 1997); *Two Parts Textbook, One Part Love* (Hyperion, 1998). Michelle Pfeiffer starred in the August 1995 box office hit *Dangerous Minds*, which was based on *My Posse Don't Do Homework*. *My Posse* and *The Girls in the Back of the Class* were both condensed in *Reader's Digest* magazine, and *Dangerous Minds* has been published in eight languages.

Johnson has presented keynote addresses to numerous organizations, including the Association of Teacher Educators, the National Council on Curriculum Development, the National School Boards Association, and the European Council of International Schools. She has conducted workshops for education students and teachers at colleges and public schools across the country. Johnson has appeared on several television shows, including *Oprah, CBS Eye to Eye, NBC Weekend Today, Tom Snyder,* and *CNN Talkback Live*.

The Queen of Education

Prologue

The Richest Country in the World— A Twenty-First-Century Fable

Once upon a time, there was a beautiful country where the children couldn't read.

"Let's create public schools to educate all of our children," said the people, "because everybody in this wonderful land of the free deserves a decent education."

And so public schools were created. And they were good. Children of all ages gathered in one room to learn reading, writing, and arithmetic. They also learned to mind their teachers—and their manners.

Some children left school after they had mastered the basics. Others stayed in school because they fell in love with books and ideas. Both groups, the temporary students and the permanent students, made contributions to their country. And the people saw that education—be it a little or a lot—was good.

Meanwhile, clever people were designing machines to make life easier. They made machines to pick cotton and cut lumber, to mow hay and pour concrete, to forge metal and create plastic. For every manual labor, they created a machine. And the country made more money and more money and more money.

One day some very clever people decided that all children should be required by law to go to school.

"More education means more money," these clever people proclaimed. "If we educate all of our children, we can become the richest country in the world. And it will be good." The clever people told the parents that their children would learn everything they needed to know in public school. The parents believed, and the law was passed, and all the children went to school.

Then a terrible war erupted, and many fathers left their homes to fight for their country. After the war the brown men who fought for their country claimed that their children should be allowed to go to the same schools as the white children. Some of the white people agreed with the brown people, but other white people disagreed and became very angry. Another miniwar erupted in the streets of the country until the government ruled that all children of all colors would attend the same schools. And whether some people liked it or not, it was good.

Then the clever people said, "Bigger is better. Look how much money we have saved by building bigger factories and putting more machines in one place." They built bigger schools and bought big yellow buses. They hired bus drivers and janitors, secretaries and maintenance people. They appointed important men in three-piece suits to supervise all of the principals who supervised all of the assistant principals who supervised all of the teachers who supervised all of the students who went to school.

But instead of allocating the money equally among all the schools, the clever people used property taxes to support the schools, so that rich children went to rich schools and poor children went to poor schools. Some people believed this disparity was unfair.

"Oh, piffle," said the clever rich people. "Poor people should be grateful that they have schools at all. Besides, if you don't tell them, they might not notice the difference." The poor people did notice, but they had no power, so their schools remained poor. And the country continued to prosper, and the people continued to have children, rich and poor, and all of the children went to school. Each year the clever people built bigger schools. Soon the schools became so big that the men in three-piece suits couldn't remember all the children's names. So they assigned each child a number. And they separated the numbers by age. And they shuffled the numbers to fit the rooms.

"We are not numbers!" the children cried. "We are little people! We don't all learn at the same pace or in the same way. We need love and compassion along with our logarithms and compositions."

"Be quiet!" shouted the clever people. "You must go to school, and there are so many of you. We must have organization, centralization, a system to keep track of you all."

And so the children were quiet, for the most part. Occasionally, one little number refused to cooperate, and he was made to stand in the corner or sent to a detention center or paddled so severely that he couldn't sit down for a week. And the other little numbers watched and listened and learned to keep their complaints to themselves. But they carved their initials into their desktops and broke the toilets in the bathrooms and smashed the windows and scrawled obscenities on the walls. They flunked their classes and claimed they didn't care. They refused to learn to read.

"If you don't earn good grades, you can't go to college," warned the clever people.

"We don't care," said the little numbers. "We don't want to go to college."

"We care," boomed the colleges. "We need students to pay tuition, or we will have to close our doors. Send us students."

And so the clever people gave the little numbers easier books to read and told the teachers to give them passing grades.

"But they should not go to college if they cannot read!" cried the teachers.

"If you were better teachers, the children would be able to read," answered the clever people. "If you want to keep your jobs, you had better learn to be team players."

And so the teachers, who had families to support and mortgages to pay, learned to play on the team and tried to ignore the sound of their hearts breaking. (Teachers who could not bring themselves to play got jobs selling insurance or shoes or washing machines.)

Many errant little numbers refused to accept the easier grades. They continued to create chaos. Some of them sneaked out of schools and hid. Some very brave stubborn students even walked out of their schools in broad daylight and dared the clever people to try to make them return.

"Education is a privilege, and you should appreciate the opportunity you have in our wonderful land of the free!" the clever people thundered. They hired people to track down the truant numbers. They built detention centers to house the numbers who continued to resist. They created special programs to rehabilitate the truants. They locked up the worst little numbers and threw away the keys.

"That will show them!" said the clever people, but it did not show them, and it was not good.

One day a very important report was published. This report compared the literacy levels of students throughout the world. And the clever people were appalled, embarrassed, enraged.

"We are the richest country in the world!" they shouted, so loudly that their faces turned purple. "We have the most television talk shows! We have the wealthiest athletes! We have the biggest schools! How can you tell us that our children cannot read? We'll show you!"

The clever people built even bigger schools. They hired more men in three-piece suits. They hired women in three-piece suits. They hired so many adults that they broke the schools' budgets.

"We need help," the clever people told the government.

"We have no money for public schools," said the powerful people (whose own children attended private schools). "We must spend billions on foreign aid and imported oil and space exploration and nuclear weapons. We have no money to educate the children of working-class people. You must help yourselves."

And so the people tried to cut the fat from the school budgets, beginning with the suits.

"Not us!" cried the suits. "We can produce scientific studies to prove that we are important. But don't worry. We will fix everything."

The suits closed many schools and consolidated others. They cut the fine arts programs from all but the richest public schools. And they opened their doors to the soft drink vendors and the candy companies that paid thousands of dollars to put their irresistible shiny machines in the schools. These things were not good at all. The children grew fatter every year, and many of them developed diabetes. With no elbow room, and without music or drawing or painting or singing to add color to their long school days, the children grew even more disruptive. Some children became cruel and tormented other children, but the schools were so huge that the people in suits didn't know the bullies' names. They couldn't catch them.

And so the students continued to complain and misbehave and escape from their educational prisons. And just like their adult counterparts, some of the little prisoners planned violent takeovers. They brought weapons into the schools and blasted their anger into the walls and the chalk boards and the teachers and their fellow little numbers.

"What is wrong with these children?" screamed the clever people. "Why don't their parents teach them to behave? Must we do everything?"

"It's television!" shouted other people.

"It's Hollywood!"

"It's sex education!" suggested some poorly educated people.

"It's the gangs!"

"It's the lack of prayer in the schools!"

"We must do something!"

And so the clever people called on the business and professional people of the richest country in the world to help them solve the problems in the public schools. Alas, in every profession, there are people who have lost sight of their mission.

"We can help," promised the profit-hungry sector of the professional people-helpers. "We know how to make people feel good about having something wrong with them."

"We can help," promised the pharmaceutical companies. "People in our country love prescription medications, especially when their insurance companies pay the bills."

"We can help too," added the advertisers. "We know how to make people buy whatever we tell them they need."

So this clever conglomerate put their heads together and came up with the most clever idea of all: there was something wrong with the children's brains! No wonder they didn't appreciate their education!

And so the clever conglomerate designed very expensive special programs and advertisements and prescription medications. They created a psychological condition and diagnosed the children who hated school. They prescribed drugs to calm those children down, to make them sit in their chairs and follow orders and not argue and not escape.

And the clever conglomerate told the parents not to worry—they were good parents. They weren't to blame for their children's misbehavior. There was something wrong with the children's brains.

And the parents were relieved and thanked the clever people for finding such a wonderful solution. And indeed, many children stopped arguing and sat in their seats and stared at their books.

But many other children refused to believe that something was wrong with their brains.

"We are not numbers! We are human beings!" they cried in despair. "If you treated us like human beings, we would show you how very smart we can be."

More and more children refused to learn to read.

"These students can learn," the clever people insisted. "They are just stubborn. But we can *make* them learn. We will give them terribly difficult tests every year, and if they do not pass the tests, they will stay in the same grade until they agree to learn."

"But we do not want to teach children to take tests!" cried the teachers. "We must teach them to read and write and think and analyze and synthesize."

"You can teach those things in your spare time—after you teach the tests," said the clever conglomerate. "And if your students don't pass the tests, then we will test *you* and show that you are incompetent. We will prove that *you* are the reason our children cannot read and our schools are mediocre."

The clever conglomerate hired professional test makers to make terribly hard tests. Children hated the tests. Teachers hated the tests. Parents hated the tests.

"We don't want to memorize facts," the children complained. "We want to use our brains. We want to think and read and write and discover and create. We don't want to learn how to take tests."

*A*nd some of the adults listened. And these compassionate adults created personal programs for the children who hated school. They spent their school budgets on students instead of adults. They called the children by name and cared about their feelings. They welcomed all students into their school—gifted and troubled, rich and poor, chocolate and vanilla, peach and caramel. Children of all ages and flavors sat side by side in the personal programs, and they thrived. They stayed in their seats and cooperated with their teachers. They learned their lessons, and they passed their exams.

"This is very, very good!" said the compassionate adults. "We must create more special personal programs. We must create whole schools that are small and personal."

And so the compassionate adults recruited other adults, and they created dozens, then hundreds, of small personal schools where students of all ages gathered and studied and were treated like human beings. And the small schools blossomed and flourished. And the clever conglomerate became jealous.

"This is not so good," whispered the members of the clever conglomerate among themselves. "We must do something!"

"We could try to be more like the small personal schools," suggested one clever person.

"What a brilliant idea!" cried the clever conglomerate. "We could treat our students with basic dignity and respect. We could create small personal programs within our big schools."

The clever conglomerate held many meetings of people wearing suits. They discussed and debated and designed and designated. They reorganized and rescheduled and researched and revised. They coordinated and delegated and overhauled and updated.

And finally, in the richest country in the world, the children began to learn to read.

The Beginning

1

The Queen of Education

I want to be crowned the queen of education. Our schools are badly broken and they must be fixed now. Somebody must take responsibility and make decisions that can be put into action immediately—no questions asked.

What qualifies me for this imperial position? Not scientific studies, not a Ph.D. thesis replete with statistical significances (although I do have some impressive pieces of university parchment and several years of experience teaching disenchanted teens). My most important queenly attribute is my passionate desire to provide a decent education for all American children.

The Queen's First Royal Edict

No classroom in this country shall have more than twenty students.

Period. We have spoken. Stop whining about the expense. Compare the figures for reducing class sizes to the figures for retaining juveniles in detention facilities and prisons. Then look at the number of illiterate incarcerated American children. It is far cheaper and much more humane to teach our children to read in school than in prison.

Teaching people to read is an important and difficult job. Alas, that is the root of the problem. Teaching is a job in the United States, when it should be a profession. Many Americans view teaching as glorified baby-sitting. We beg to differ. Even if you aren't a trained teacher, you may stand in a teacher's shoes (we suggest comfortable rubber soles). Take any subject. Now sit down and create a plan for teaching said subject to people who know nothing about this topic and who vehemently prefer to remain ignorant. Figure out how to make these people listen to you, make them desire this knowledge. Next implement your plan in a location that is extremely cold or unbearably hot, with poor ventilation and with flickering fluorescents overhead, in a room furnished with bun-numbing unpadded plastic chairs. Ensure that at least one each of the following personalities is included among the recalcitrant recipients of your wisdom: bully, gangster, drug dealer, drug addict, drunkard, sexually abused person, starving person, and a person who simply cannot sit still. And ensure that you have more students than you have seats or lesson books.

Even if you have performed this teaching experiment only in your ever-expanding mind, you will surely support

The Queen's Second Royal Edict

Every elected representative in this country, from the tiniest town to the U.S. Congress, must spend two weeks in the public school classroom, teaching from the curriculum and materials available and living on a teacher's salary for those two weeks.

No limos, no catered meals, no two-hour three-martini lunches. Marvelous things will happen. First, our lawmakers will fall in love with our children, just as we teachers do, and they will see that most American children are not apathetic amoral sex-crazed gangster wanna-bes. They will see that our children are good little people, desperately in need of good big leaders.

Second, politicians will realize that teaching well is darned difficult, time-consuming, emotionally draining work and that paying teachers such paltry sums is insulting and unethical. They will introduce legislation to double teachers' salaries and triple education budgets. Never again will teachers have to beg for books and paper. Not bad for our first day's work.

The Queen's Third Royal Edict

Every member of Congress shall enroll his or her children in the poorest public school located in the representative's home district for at least one semester each year.

Thus, our lawmakers shall demonstrate their faith in the quality of education in our country. And they will be inclined to improve public education and solve school-related problems in a humane, timely, and efficient manner. School safety and effectiveness will become a priority among our elected officials just as it is among the working classes. This measure will also help bridge the ever-growing gap between rich and poor Americans.

The Queen's Fourth Royal Edict

Begin to deflate the bureaucratic bloat in our public school system this very instant.

Starting at the top of every educational hierarchy composed of nonteaching personnel (such as the U.S. Department of Education, state departments of education, district superintendent offices, and so on), the head honcho shall be sent home for one week. Secretaries, assistants, and executive aides will operate schools—as they normally do. If things are running smoothly at the end of the week, the head honcho's position shall be eliminated. Half of the former honcho's salary must go directly to purchase student materials for the school library and reading programs, because reading is the foundation for all academic achievement. The other half of the saved salary shall be evenly divided among the employees on the lowest pay scale in that particular school system: secretaries, classroom aides, custodial staff, and so on.

On to the second-highest honcho, and the third, moving down the administrative food chain until each school's vital and necessary positions have been identified, at which time they shall be filled with qualified and experienced former classroom teachers.

The queen eagerly anticipates the emergence of lean and muscular school systems, free from the deadening weight and gaseous bloat of overadministration.

The Queen's Fifth Royal Edict

Common sense shall take priority in addressing problems and challenges in our schools.

Common-sense solutions shall be implemented before any monies are spent on research or statistical studies. Take the question of whether to reduce class sizes. Anybody with a smidgen of common sense can see that smaller classes (such as those in any reputable private school) result in more personal attention for students; this in turn results in accelerated learning, higher test scores, and fewer behavior problems.

In cases where the common-sense solution may not be so obvious, school boards and administrators shall put the question to the queen's common-sense test (QCST). The QCST consists of the following: ask a Native American medicine woman, an ace auto mechanic, an at-risk teenager, and a four-year-old child for their opinions. None of those people stands to benefit financially or politically from decisions involving our schools, and each may offer a unique and instructive perspective. The medicine woman will consider the spiritual aspect of the problem without the pressure of organized religious bias. The mechanic will look at the logistics. The at-risk teen will provide a youthful perspective and may point out past mistakes. And the child will tell the truth.

We realize that some of you are shaking your heads at this point, and we understand your concern. The QCST may sound ridiculous and frivolous at first, but consider another test question: Should restless, fidgety young children be given prescription drugs as a first resort to calm them down? The medicine woman would most likely suggest trying a natural remedy. The mechanic would point out that medicating children is like applying duct tape to a cracked radiator hose—it may provide a temporary solution but may create a more expensive and damaging problem later on. The at-risk teen will surely suggest many nonmedical reasons why a child might not be able to concentrate in school. And the child would find the question incomprehensible.

The following questions shall be put to the QCST immediately:

Should physical education programs be a top priority in a nation where childhood obesity and diabetes have reached epidemic proportions?

Should fine arts programs be sacrificed to save money, although children universally love and respond to music, dance, drawing, painting, sculpting, and theater?

Does sentencing students to detention or suspension effectively alter their behavior and attitudes, resulting in academic achievement?

And thus we arrive at

The Queen's Sixth Royal Edict

In every instance in which common sense can address a problem, money that a school district would have spent on academic research and statistical studies shall go directly to student libraries, incandescent lighting for classrooms, and fine arts programs.

The Queen's Seventh Royal Edict

Stop the testing frenzy. Cease the accountability testing of licensed teachers and the relentless testing of children.

Accountability is a good idea, but testing teachers after licensing them is illogical, if not insane. Would anybody suggest first hiring surgeons, dentists, or air traffic controllers and *then* creating elaborate schemes to test their skills? Surely not. We know that if these professionals fail to do their jobs, people shall be badly injured or killed, so we test them before they start their training and again before licensing them to begin work. Students shan't die if teachers are inept, but illiteracy can cause extreme pain and suffering to our country as well as our children. Let us treat teachers as we do other certificated professionals: test them before they start training; test them after they finish training; then license them, trust them, and let them perform their important work.

Most American teachers do good work, but alas, some don't. However, the queen is convinced that ineffective teachers teach poorly not because they lack intelligence or desire but because they lack the proper training. If we must hold someone accountable for our teachers' effectiveness, we must look to our teacher-training institutions. We must hold them accountable for the preparedness of the teachers they train and license.

Educating our children is as important as performing brain surgery, seeking justice in the courts, or running a profitable business. Therefore, the queen maintains that earning acceptance to a college of education should be as difficult as earning acceptance to an esteemed medical school, law school, or MBA program—and equally difficult to complete. We must ensure that when our teachers receive their licenses, they are adequately prepared to perform as professional educators.

The queen shall establish rigorous entrance requirements for education programs: comprehensive academic exams to ensure that teachers know their subjects; psychological exams to screen out potential child molesters; and practical demonstrations of ability to ensure that our intelligent, educated, psychologically well-adjusted teachers can actually teach (unfortunately, intelligence, education, and desire do not automatically enable someone to teach).

The queen also shall require that teacher candidates, once accepted, shall receive an excellent education in theoretical and practical courses, including child and adolescent psychology, leadership, motivation, classroom management, and conflict resolution—

all taught by people who have hands-on experience in public school classrooms. Teachers shall also be required to learn at least one foreign language; thus, they will be able to effectively teach a wider range of students, and they will gain a new compassion and tolerance for children who struggle to learn new concepts and skills presented in a language that is not their native tongue.

We shall require a B average for education coursework and an intensive year-long internship, closely supervised by experienced professionals, followed by a rigorous exit exam evaluated by a committee of objective, knowledgeable experts. (If a teacher candidate cannot pass the exit exam, the education program shall issue no license, even if there is a shortage of teachers. We don't grant medical licenses simply because we need doctors and dentists.) And teachers, like other professionals, must periodically requalify for their licenses.

We should like to suggest at this point a fitting new title for our qualified, rigorously tested, dedicated, effective teachers: public school professors. And may we also suggest an appropriate new starting salary equal to the salaries of other licensed professionals with five years of challenging academic training: a minimum entry-level salary equal to that of other professionals in business, medicine, and law.

Well-trained teachers know how to motivate. They know how to lead. They know how to teach. And when teachers teach, students learn. Attitudes and behavior improve. Achievement soars. And the demand for standardized tests-tests-tests-tests disappears. The queen finds constant testing quite tiresome, and we are not convinced that true academic progress can be evaluated with a standardized exam, particularly an exam that is graded by a machine.

The queen does acknowledge that some tests are necessary, however. Every time we meet a dean of an education college, we ask, "Are your teacher candidates tested for psychological fitness? Do you know why your education students want to be teachers? Do you ask whether your candidates even like children?" The answer, sadly, invariably, is "no."

Americans have a ludicrously democratic approach to training teachers: anyone who wants to be a teacher can enter a teacher-training program. Americans assume that being educated automatically enables a person to teach effectively and that teachers want to teach. However, the queen conducted an unofficial survey when we first began teaching, and the responses left us aghast:

- "I want my summers off."
- "I want to work the same hours as my spouse."
- "I want the same vacation days as my children."
- "I earned the degree. Now I must teach until I can find another job."

Some people find these reasons acceptable. Her Majesty does not. We wonder. Would these same reasonable people let a surgeon apply a scalpel to their skulls if she said, "I became a brain surgeon so that I could have Fridays off to golf"? We think not. Thus, the need for psychological screening of potential teachers.

We are pleased. We have elevated teaching to a well-paid profession, adequately trained our teachers, reduced class sizes to facilitate learning, ensured that our teacher candidates want to teach and that they are not child molesters. How very excellent. These steps shall eliminate some huge problems such as forcing teachers to spend inordinate amounts of time teaching to the tests instead of teaching students to think. (Mr. President, if you want to know if a child can read, you must take time to listen to the child read.) We will not have a teacher shortage because young people will want to become public school professors; they will want to enjoy the job satisfaction, prestige, and compensation that teachers receive.

Oh, my. The realists, the perennially practical among us are raising their hands. Yes, it will be difficult to find a university willing to turn away potential teachers who don't meet the new, improved entrance requirements. Turning away students means turning away money, and universities are understandably averse to such behavior. But certainly in this great nation of big business, of corporate multimillionaires, we could find one company or corporation or cartel whose intelligent, compassionate, and ethical CEO believes in education and appreciates good public relations. This savvy CEO can approve funding for the academic program and salaries of our initial group of crackerjack teachers. When that first class of bright, passionate, capable, supremely qualified public school professors strides to the head of the class, the students will respond; the CEO will receive another million dollars in stock incentives; and the rest will be history.

The queen is ready. We stand by our throne, tiara freshly polished, waiting. God save our schools.

2

Questions That Keep Me Awake at Night

Why do so many schools sell our children's health to the highest bidder, signing multimillion dollar contracts to place soda and candy machines in our schools when millions of children suffer from diabetes and obesity? Doesn't that make about as much sense as placing beer machines in the workplaces of adult alcoholics?

Why do we insist that all children learn to read at the same age, whether they are ready or not? Clearly, this practice creates lifelong nonreaders. So why can't we teach children to read when they are ready?

Why do many politicians believe that sitting amidst a group of children and reading a story aloud is equivalent to teaching?

Why do schools put so much focus on student attendance, when those same schools often have no hot water, soap, or paper towels for students to wash their hands—the primary method of preventing the spread of colds and flu that keep kids out of school in the first place?

Why do we insist on grading children on their reading ability while they are still learning to read—so that reading becomes a competition and a chore instead of a joy? Although testing children is necessary to make sure they are progressing, why is it so important to assign a grade to tiny children who are struggling to learn one of the most important skills of their lives?

How many children would yearn to ride a bike if they were graded on their ability to steer and pedal, and pitted against their peers as they were learning?

Why can a stranger walk into so many public schools without being questioned when the same person could not even step into the elevator in any major law office, brokerage firm, or bank without being detained, questioned, diverted, restrained, or—at the very least—photographed by a security camera?

Why are most decisions concerning school operations based on ease of administration, scheduling, testing, or some other factor that will make life easier for adults instead of on what is truly best for our children?

Why do we hire so many people who have never been classroom teachers to supervise entire school districts?

Why do we make passing periods in high schools so short, then punish students who are ten seconds tardy because they stopped to use the restroom, fetch forgotten materials from their lockers, or say hello to a dear friend?

Instead of making passing periods short so that students won't have time to hurt each other, why don't we do something to stop the harassment and bullying that pervade our schools?

Why do working-class voters keep supporting lawmakers who refuse to send their own children to public schools, especially when those same lawmakers raise their own salaries and then cut the budgets for public schools?

Why do we insist that all class periods be the same length when some subjects clearly take more time to teach and to learn?

Why does every teacher in a school have to have the same number of students per class? Doesn't teaching a difficult and important subject such as reading merit smaller classes in which students can receive individual attention—so that we can make sure we truly leave no child behind?

Why don't we establish a nationwide salary schedule for public school teachers?

Why do we allow school boards—often composed of people completely untrained in teaching or child psychology—to create policy and procedures for our schools? Do we place any comparable public service in the hands of complete amateurs?

Why don't principals teach anymore?

Why do we insist on age-based grouping, when it causes so many problems, given the vastly differing rates of mental, emotional, and physical development among children? Wouldn't it make more sense to teach prealgebra to children when their brains are ready to accept abstract concepts, instead of forcing them to take it before they are ready, making it a requirement for graduation, and then failing them?

Why does it matter whether children have rings in their navels or nostrils if they behave themselves and earn good grades?

Why do so many adults believe that making students sit and suffer when they need to use the restroom will teach them self-control? How many adults would remain at jobs where they were not permitted to use the restroom without forfeiting pay or benefits?

Why do we allow students who are receiving a free education (and their parents) to sue public schools when we do not permit members of the military who risk their lives to defend their country to sue the government? Shouldn't lawsuits against individual school districts be limited to cases wherein children are sexually abused, severely injured, or killed due to gross negligence on the part of school staff members? Shouldn't parents whose children are intentionally injured by other children be required to sue the students (or parents) who performed the assault, instead of the school system where such assaults are prohibited and punished?

Why do people expect children to be respectful when we treat them with so little respect?

Why do people find it acceptable for a school district to eliminate fine arts programs, limp along with one or two computers in the library, issue outdated textbooks, and cram thirty-five or forty students into one classroom—and then allocate money from what the district calls a different budget to resurface the football field or refurbish the carpet in the district superintendent's office?

Why do children have to attend school during hours that are convenient for the business community? Why don't we base our school hours on the actual time needed to acquire knowledge and master skills?

Why does our society blame children when a teacher is unable to teach them?

Why can't the United States follow the example of countries that provide preschool and day care for all children, so that school schedules don't have to be locked to parent work schedules?

Why are school buildings so ugly? Is there a law that says schools must sport gray linoleum and prison-style architecture?

Why do so many new schools have windows that don't open, so that children are forced to breathe recycled air all day long?

Why do school districts assign twenty-five, thirty, or more tiny children, each with a unique learning style and rate of mental development, to one classroom and then expect one teacher to teach all those tiny children to read?

Why don't we make our schools places where children want to be if we truly want to increase attendance?

Why don't we stop teachers and administrators from humiliating students? And then stop those same students—who have learned by example—to stop humiliating other students?

Why do so many people believe that you can accurately assess a child's knowledge or skills by asking questions that can be answered on a Scantron form and graded by a machine?

Why have we let litigious people spoil things for so many children who now cannot go on field trips or play in their school gyms on rainy Saturday afternoons because school districts are held hostage by the fear of frivolous lawsuits? Shouldn't a parent permission slip be just that—permission to engage in an activity with the understanding that sometimes children get hurt and that a school is not legally responsible for injuries except in the case of clear and gross negligence by a staff member?

Why does the United States use 85 percent of the world's supply of methylphenidate (Ritalin, Concerta, etc.)?

Why, oh why, oh why don't we ask what our children are eating and drinking, how much they are sleeping, and what kind of lighting and air they are exposed to in school, before we medicate three million of them in an effort to make them sit down and be quiet?

Why can't we focus on making our schools safe and teaching children how to behave, instead of building schools that try to avoid student conflicts by not allowing the study body to assemble in one place? Why can't we teach our children to conduct themselves with self-respect in public, instead of eliminating auditoriums so student-body assembles, award ceremonies, or entertainment are impossible?

Why do we continue to consolidate schools and create bigger campuses when we can clearly see that bigger schools have bigger problems and that students thrive in smaller, community-based schools where they receive individual attention and feel more at home?

Why does the government pay schools to label children as special ed, attention deficit hyperactivity disordered, developmentally delayed, emotionally disturbed, and so on? Doesn't this increase the possibility that children will be mislabeled, misdiagnosed, and mistaught?

Why can't we call stubborn students stubborn and angry students angry instead of implying that they suffer from a mental or emotional disorder that makes them defy authority?

Why do so many schools suspend or expel children for using the same foul language at school that those children routinely hear in movies, on television, and sometimes in their own homes?

Why does our society offer dynamic, successful teachers so much more money to talk or write or teach about teaching than to teach children? Why does our society believe it is acceptable to offer an experienced, effective teacher a lower salary than any company would offer an entry-level executive secretary?

Why can our country afford hundreds of billions of dollars to aid foreign countries and yet not be able to afford to fix our own ramshackle public schools?

3

The Accidental Teacher

I never wanted to be a high school teacher. My plan, from the day Mrs. Hodak published my first poem in our fifth-grade class newspaper, *The Writer's Cramp*, was to become a novelist and college professor. But life has a way of sneaking up behind me and spinning me around so that I end up traveling in a different direction.

When I graduated from high school, I was academically accomplished but socially retarded. Aside from staying with my grandmother and two close friends from church, I had never spent the night away from home. I had been to a movie theater twice and to a restaurant once, and I had seen one black person. I believed that girls were supposed to save themselves for marriage and that if you worked hard and played fair, you would live a wonderful life and go straight to heaven when you died.

The only one of the five children in our family who cared enough about going to college to find a way to pay the tuition, I secured a student loan and shuffled off to Indiana University of Pennsylvania, whose college campus was larger than my hometown, Youngsville, Pennsylvania, "The Biggest Little Town on the Map." More students were enrolled in my biology class at college than had been enrolled in my entire high school back home, so I was a little overwhelmed at first, but I was determined to stay until I had earned my Ph.D.

Forty-five days into my college career, a throng of boys burst into the girls' dorm and shouted, "Frat party! Frat party! You're all invited!" I had been to one or two parties in my day, so I knew what people did at parties—they ate chips and soda, which we had not been allowed to imbibe in my boringly wholesome childhood home. I followed a group of girls out of the dorm and down the street. Indeed, the moment I entered the frat house, a boy handed me a Coke. I didn't know you could put alcohol in Coca-Cola, so after a quick sip, I handed the glass back.

"There's something wrong with this soda," I said. "I think it's gone bad."

"No, honey, that's good," he said. "You drink it."

So I did, and it was good. Then someone shouted, "Who wants to see a movie?"

I was thrilled. The movie theater in Youngsville had closed when I was a small child, and the nearby drive-in theater closed a few years later. Television was still black and white and still viewed with a great deal of suspicion by my father when I was a teen, so I had seen only a few movies in my life, classics such as *Sleeping Beauty* and *It's a Wonderful Life*. *College is a wonderful place*, I thought, as I followed a group of people upstairs to a room where a white sheet was tacked on a wall and a movie projector was whirring in the corner. The movie was black-and-white and quite blurry, so I sat down right in front of the sheet, where I could get a good view. After a few minutes, when my eyes had adjusted, I realized I was looking at a naked woman holding a snake. I had no idea what she planned to do with the snake, but I knew my Grandma Lauffenberger would have a heart attack if she ever found out I was in that room.

I jumped to my feet and raced down the hall. A very tall young man followed me. I didn't know him and had never spoken to him, so the only explanation I can find is that he had noticed me sitting right in front of the movie and had thought, *Cool. Hot chick. She's into porn.*

The tall young man and I both ran into a bedroom, where he promptly threw me down on a bed and pounced on me. Perhaps he thought he was being romantic, but I did not. And I grew up out in the country with two large brothers who taught me how to "rassle"—so I hurt that tall young frat boy. Not permanently. I'm sure he could still have children. But that day he learned that you do not kiss a Johnson girl if she doesn't want you to. And I learned that I had much to learn before I was prepared to earn my Ph.D. I ran back to the dorm, packed my bags, got on a bus that took me as near to Youngsville as it possibly could. Then I called my mother.

"Honey, what are you doing?" she asked. "You're supposed to be going to college."

"Mama," I said, "I don't know how to go to college."

Mama Johnson came to fetch me in our old green Oldsmobile station wagon. I never told her or anybody else about the frat party, and nobody asked why I had returned to Youngsville. They all assumed that I had learned my lesson, gallivanting around the country, wasting all that money on who knows what. I wondered whether the incident was my wake-up call, a warning that rampant socializing and drinking alcohol would lead me straight to ruin.

After I had been at home a few weeks, I decided I would become an actress first and a professor and novelist later on, after I had more life experience. I intended to enroll in the off-campus division of Edinboro State College in Warren, where I would audition for a role in the upcoming production of *You're a Good Man, Charlie Brown*. I announced my decision at the dinner table, inspiring my father to stop chewing his meatloaf and whack the table with his fist.

"No daughter of mine is going to be an actress," he thundered in his thunderous fatherly manner. "Actors are all prostitutes and drug addicts."

Another solid whack on the table top indicated the end of the discussion.

"OK, Daddy," I said. "I'll get a job instead."

My father pointed the business end of his fork at me to indicate that I should wait for him to swallow his mouthful of meatloaf before speaking further.

"You don't need money," he said. "You need to settle down, find a good man. Get married, have babies like a normal woman."

"That's why I want a job," I said. "I want to save money for my wedding someday."

"Hnh." My father nodded, satisfied that he had talked some sense into me.

So I got a job as a waitress at a pizza parlor in Warren, rented a cheesy studio apartment, and enrolled in the off-campus division of Edinboro State College, where I auditioned for a role in *You're a Good Man, Charlie Brown*. The director chose me to play Lucy, and I called to warn my mother, who agreed to hide the newspaper when the production dates were announced.

One of the welders at Betts Machine, where my father was foreman, must have read the paper because a few days after the final curtain of the last show, my father showed up at my apartment with his pickup truck. He threw everything I owned into the back, threw me into the front, and drove me down Jackson Run and up the dirt road through Chandler's Valley to the top of Brown Hill, where my mother stood watching from the kitchen doorway, twisting her apron in her hands.

"You're going to stay in this house and behave yourself until you are twenty-one or until you come to your senses," my father said. He clomped into the living room and lowered his aching back into his easy chair, which meant that he had said all he was going to say on the subject.

A few weeks later, as I sat warming my frosty toes by the woodstove in the back room, gazing out the window at a swirly snowstorm, plotting my next escape, my mother came in from the kitchen and handed me a brochure.

"Look at this, honey," she said. "They've got girls doing all kinds of jobs, driving airplanes and everything."

I laughed.

"I'm serious," my mother said. "I know you want to be a writer and a college professor, but it says here that you could be a journalist. They would pay for your college too, and you would have a chance to travel." She looked up from her reading and smiled. I can still see her face, her bright red lipstick and black plastic cat-eye glasses with one tasteful rhinestone in the little point at the tip of the frame on each side.

"It says it wouldn't be just a job, honey; it would be an adventure."

And so, one Saturday afternoon while my father was busy doing chores in the barn, my mother drove me to the bus station and I rolled off to join the navy—the last time I took my mother's advice. I did learn to be a journalist in the navy, and I learned a lot of other things as well, in addition to shoe shining, deck swabbing, and an impressive array of swearwords. As a broadcast specialist, I was stationed at Clark Air Base in the Philippines for three years, where I lived with a Filipino family in the barrio of Old Balibago during much of that time. I learned how to speak a little Tagalog (*maganda ka*) and how to cook *pancit* and *lumpia*. I learned how it feels to be unable to speak the language that everybody else in the community speaks and how difficult learning a new language is. I learned how it feels to be the only person in town with my skin color. Even though the Filipinos were kind to me, I felt uncomfortable, as though something were wrong with me.

After two more tries, I finally learned how to go to college. I got my bachelor's degree in psychology, after which my military superiors strongly encouraged me to become an officer. I believe the idea is that if you are enlisted and well educated, you might start asking questions that would undermine your superiors' authority and hinder your willingness to follow orders without considering whether there might perhaps be a better option.

I reported to navy officer candidate school (OCS) in Newport, Rhode Island, in mid-November after having lived in the Philippines, where 75 degrees feels cold enough to make a person put on a warm jacket. I promptly developed a stubborn case of hypothermia, and one of my workout partners, a marine corps major, suggested that I might transfer to marine corps OCS. A few weeks later, I was in Quantico, Virginia, wearing a down jacket, heavy gloves, two pairs of wool socks, and a toasty cap. I remember thinking to myself, *These guys may shave their heads and lift weights until they develop pectorals that women would die for, but they know how to dress in the winter.* And so I marched and sang and marched and jogged and marched and dismantled howitzers and marched and survived the endurance course and marched and ate C-rats and marched and fired M16s from standing, kneeling, and lying positions. And by the time my brain thawed, I was a second lieutenant, yes, ma'am.

When I turned twenty-eight, I stepped back to take a look at my life and realized I had never been a free woman. I had gone directly from my father's domain to the navy to the marines, and all three organizations were remarkably similar. I had never been in a position to make even simple decisions about my own life, such as what to wear. My father and the military both issued and enforced strict rules and regulations regarding the proper behavior of women, such as the rule that required at least half of a woman's kneecaps to be covered by her skirt lest the world glimpse her naked knees and mistake her for a shameless hussy. So I decided to try civilian life and get back on track toward earning that Ph.D. I bought a pink sweater, some short skirts, some dangly earrings, and a completely frivolous old yellow Fiat convertible. Then I assessed my talents. I thought, *Let's see. I'm trained in writing, weapons, and hand-to-hand combat. Perfect—I'll teach high school!*

Seriously, I kept reading reports about American teenagers who graduated from high school although they couldn't read. I decided that I would teach high school while I was a graduate student. My students would know how to read, and I would have a better idea of what my students would be like as a college professor.

While I was still working on my master's, before I had a chance to do any student teaching, I was offered a job as a teaching intern. I would be paid, and I would not be directly supervised. After nine years in the military, I had had enough supervision. And as a grad student, I needed the money. My job, they explained, would be to teach one section of regular sophomore English.

A piece of cake. I couldn't wait to share my love of literature with my students.

Unfortunately, my students were not even minutely interested in literature. They didn't seem to be interested in me either, although I firmly announced several times that it was time to settle down and open our books. Most of the students were seated, but few were facing forward, and nearly all of them were talking.

Thinking that perhaps they might quiet down if I wrote my name on the board as an introduction, I turned and picked up a piece of chalk. A second later a thick red schoolhouse dictionary flew from the back of the room and bounced off the chalkboard, missing my head by about two inches. I turned around and saw a group of boys standing in the back of the room, arms crossed over their chests, glaring at me.

Perhaps it's me, I thought. If I had gone the standard route to teaching by majoring in education as an undergraduate, perhaps I would have taken the course that covered mutiny and book hurling. Although I outranked the kids, they didn't recognize my authority, so issuing orders wouldn't work. So I did what seemed to be the most logical thing to do under the circumstances: I walked out of the classroom.

Behind me I could hear students cheering as I headed down the walkway to Hal Black's room. An Army vet and my mentor, Hal had been teaching for nearly thirty years. He would know what to do. Hal, who was about as white as a white man can get, answered the door wearing a T-shirt that proclaimed: It's a Black Thing.

"Is my class truly what you call regular?" I asked.

"Not exactly," Hal said. He explained that my class was exceptional in a couple of ways: they had driven their regular teacher out of the room in tears so many times that she had called the office one Friday and announced that she was retiring the following Monday. The substitutes who had taught her class were not inclined to return more than once or twice. And so the students were under the impression that they were ruthless, one of their favorite adjectives.

"You'd better do something fast," Hal said as he closed the door softly in my face. I thought of running very fast to my car to go get a real job, but I was a psych major and naturally stubborn. Thirty-four kids in that classroom *hadn't* thrown a book. Why desert them? And the boy who had thrown the book must have had a reason. Most teenagers aren't psychotic, although many act as though they are. So if the boy was not mentally ill, then why had he hurled the dictionary at me, knowing that the consequences would be severe? Why bother going to school if you are going to throw a book at a teacher? Clearly, his act was a challenge to my authority. But I sensed that it was more than a simple challenge. He wanted out of my classroom, even if it meant detention, suspension, or expulsion. But why did he want out of my room? Perhaps he had to use the restroom and was embarrassed to ask a woman. Perhaps he wanted to meet his girlfriend or smoke a cigarette or buy some recreational drugs. Or perhaps he couldn't read and would rather be punished than humiliated. If he deliberately brought the punishment upon himself, then he could claim he didn't care.

Facing belligerent boys was nothing new for me. Back in 1972, when I enlisted in the navy, I met plenty of sailors who didn't relish the idea of women in "this man's navy." Those swabbies made me cry at least once a day for the first six months of my enlistment. They tormented me until finally it dawned on me that they were just like my brothers: they would keep tormenting me as long as I kept crying. So I learned how to act like I didn't care—and I learned it very convincingly. And when I walked back into that classroom and looked at the boy who had thrown the dictionary at my head, I could see that he was a pretty good little actor. But I knew exactly what he was doing. I knew he was angry and scared. I knew he cared about school because he was there. If he truly didn't care about school, he wouldn't bother to come and cause trouble.

When I pushed the door open, the students were surprised to see me, so they were momentarily quiet. I was wearing cowboy boots at the time, which created a very nice sound effect as I marched across the tile floor toward my dictionary-throwing pupil. (I recommend to new teachers that they wear boots. They create a very solid authoritative thunking sound, much more than the clickety-click of high heels or the squish-squash of rubber-soled sneakers.)

I approached the young man until we stood face to face, his back against the wall. Taking a tip from my military drill instructors, I stood as close as possible to the boy, so that if he breathed he would touch me—and I knew that touching a teacher was not likely to be high on his list of acceptable activities. We stood toe to toe, staring each other down. He had youth and determination on his side, but I had age and experience on mine. I knew I could stand at attention for two hours if necessary, and I knew that he wouldn't last more than a few minutes.

Although drill instructors never reveal their secrets to those of us who haven't earned the right to wear a Smokey, I believe I know what they are thinking when they stare at a scared recruit: *I am going to rip your heart out and eat it raw.* Or something along those lines. Thinking such things gives you a certain look, even without the official intimidating hat. And so that is what I thought as I stared at my young challenger. After a few minutes, I could see the sweat come out on his upper lip. Trying my best to sound ruthless, I said, "I would appreciate it, young man, if you would sit down. Right now." And he did!

I don't know who was more surprised. At that moment it occurred to me that all the teacher training in the world wouldn't help until I could connect with my students. So I said, "Thank you very much, young man," and marched to the front of the room, where I announced, "I'm too young to retire and too mean to quit, so sit down and shut up because you have a teacher, and I'm here to stay. I intend to teach this class."

One of the boys raised his arm and chugged the air, yelling, "Kick butt! Kick butt!"

"Darned straight I will kick some butt," I said. "You see that door you walked in when you came to this class? That door works both ways. If you want to be an ignorant failure, you can walk right back out that door. Don't waste my time or yours by coming into this room if you don't want to learn. I am here to help you become successful people. I am not here to boss you around. If I wanted to boss people around, I would have stayed in the military, where it would have been much easier. I will never humiliate you; I will never embarrass you; and I will never, ever force you to read out loud because I know adults who would quit their jobs if they had to read out loud when they went to work. But I will require that you think. And if anybody dies from that, I will take full responsibility for your death."

Apparently, nobody had ever stated the case for education in quite that manner because they were speechless for a few moments. Everybody sat in a desk, and nobody threw anything at me for the next hour. I was encouraged enough to return the following day—and so were they.

Before long the subject of grades raised its grisly head. I explained to my students that if they wanted to pass, all they had to do was work as hard as they needed to work, depending on their natural ability, academic skills, and determination.

One girl shook her head and sighed dramatically.

"It don't matter what we do," she said, "because Miss Shepard done flunked us all. She wrote a red F in the grade book—in ink."

Her classmates nodded, and the expressions on their faces clearly said: *There you are. A red F. In ink. In the official grade book.*

It might as well be carved in stone. Why bother trying when we have already failed?

"Well, that doesn't seem fair, and I don't have Miss Shepard's grade book," I said. "So as far as I'm concerned, everybody has an A right now, and I am writing it in my grade book in red ink."

I opened my grade book and begin writing large red As in the spaces beside their names. I could feel the dynamic in that classroom change. Every single student in that class was riveted. Collectively, they held their breath. I could actually feel the hope fluttering in their hearts.

Then from the back of the room, I heard a boy whisper, "She's lyin'."

The boy beside him whispered, much louder, "Shut up! What if she ain't lying? I ain't never had an A before."

And thus my basic teaching philosophy was born:

> When students believe that success is possible, they will try. If they don't believe success is possible, no matter how easy the material or how smart the student, they will fail.

That was lesson number one from my supposedly unteachable students (all of whom decided to pass that class).

I don't mean to imply that teaching became effortless after that day or that I never faced failures, because I had my share, but those failures were not due to antagonism between my students and me or because they lacked the motivation to try. Once I established that I was truly on their side and that my goal was to help them succeed and not to defeat them, most of my students felt confident enough to at least try to do their assignments and homework, some for the first time in their lives. The holdouts required more effort on my part, and I chose private journals as a way to bridge the communications gap for a number of reasons: handwriting clues, anonymity, and permanence.

Even an amateur handwriting analyst can find clues to student personalities in their writing. Children with very low self-esteem, for example, will often write in very tiny, cramped letters, with a light hand, as though they wish they could be invisible. Students who are dyslexic will often switch letters around or omit words from their sentences. Creative students who are apt to be kinesthetic learners may ignore margins or embellish their writing with cartoons, symbols, or illustrations.

Anonymity was my students' idea. When I asked them to write in their journals, several complained that they didn't want to write "personal stuff" that I would read and use against them. I promised that unless I believed they were going to hurt themselves or somebody else, I would never reveal the contents of their private journals, even to their parents or the principal. On to their next objection: they would flunk because their grammar and spelling sucked.

"I will grade the journals on content only," I promised. "I want you to concentrate on developing your thoughts and expressing your ideas. No dinks for grammar or spelling—you can always fix those things. I'd rather read something rough and compelling than a perfectly grammatical, perfectly boring little essay about nothing."

"You mean this is English class and you aren't going to grade spelling and grammar?" one girl asked, her voice brimming with suspicion.

"When we do grammar exercises or spelling tests, then I'll grade them, but your journals are exempt. When it's time to write a formal essay, you can take something from your journal and fix it up, correct the grammar and spelling, and turn it in for a grade."

OK, this was starting to sound good to them. About half of my students seemed willing to try. But then a boy in the back wanted to know what would happen if they did write personal things and then somebody else stole their journal and shared their innermost thoughts with their cruel and vicious peer group. I promised to guarantee anonymity by marking each journal with a special code on the back. Only the student and I would know that code. That way, if the journal were lost or stolen, nobody would know the name of the author. And I would post a notice in writing that categorized journal stealing (including reading over somebody's shoulder without their permission) as a class F felony, punishable by the worst things I could legally do to them and some illegal things I could do without getting caught. I promised that any journal snitchers would deeply regret their snitching when I got my hands on them.

"You mean you'd do something that might get you in trouble just because I stole somebody's journal?" the boy asked.

"Yes," I said. "Because I think it's that important for you to be able to express yourself honestly without worrying about retaliation of some kind."

"And you'd be, like, really pissed at me and you'd get even?"

"Well, yes," I said.

"That's cool," the boy said, and his classmates agreed. And so we began journal writing. Every day I gave them a choice of prompts, and they were to write one full page. One day's prompts might include the following:

1. Tell about a time you told a big lie and got caught.

2. Write a letter to your parents, telling them what a good or bad job they are doing in raising you. (You can tear up the letter after you write it.)

3. What makes you so mad you could spit?

4. Tell me about the best or worst teacher you ever had.

5. Describe the best or worst day of your life.

If students couldn't write about any of my prompts, they could choose their own topic, as long as they truly had something to say.

"Don't write me a page about how you're going to eat pizza for lunch," I warned. "Write something worth reading. Develop your ideas. I'm looking for some brain power."

If they decided after writing that their journal entry was too personal and they didn't want me to read it, then they could fold that page in half so that the writing didn't show; I gave my word of honor that I would turn up one corner just to see that the page had writing but I would not read the entry. For several weeks I kept my word, and then one day a boy who rarely spoke to anybody, including me, and who rarely wrote more than a few sentences sat and scribbled away even after the journal-writing time ended. I was eager to read his journal, hoping that perhaps I had finally made a connection. That night, when I opened the journal and found the page folded over, I couldn't resist. I opened the page. There were shreds where a page had been ripped out of the notebook and one sentence scrawled across the folded page: "I knew I couldn't trust you, you fucking liar." That was the first and last time I read anything I had promised not to read.

The original purpose of the journals had been to convince my students to believe that they had something to say, to free them from the constraints of spelling and grammar, to let me see how much they really knew about critical thinking and writing. But those first journals gave me so much insight into student behavior that I made journal writing a standard in my classroom. I developed a reputation for successfully teaching so-called "unteachable" kids, and during the next four years, I taught hundreds of them. And through their journals, those students taught me the most important lesson I have ever learned about teaching:

> There is a reason for everything a child does. And until you understand the reason for the behavior, you cannot expect to make a permanent change.

I would like to share just three of the many examples of student behavior that seemed illogical to me until I learned, through the journals, what caused the behavior.

During her first year in our at-risk program, Tyeisha filled her journal with page after page about how much fun it was to be a cheerleader and where she planned to go to college and how many children she intended to have when she was happily married. The second year Tyeisha scrawled obscenities or sat with her arms crossed during journal-writing periods. She refused to do her class-work, fought with her fellow classmates, and defied every one of the teachers in the program's team. We exhausted our repertoire of repercussions—demerits, lunch detention, parent conferences, office referrals, suspension—but the bad behavior continued. The only time there was a brief respite was immediately after a parent conference. I thought more conferences might help, but then I learned that Tyeisha's parents were divorced; both had remarried, and her father lived some distance away. In order to come to a conference, he had to take time off work and drive for several hours.

"Do you miss your father?" I wrote in Tyeisha's journal that night. When I handed her the journal the following day, she slammed it on her desk without opening it. I gently opened it to the page with my question and walked away.

Tyeisha wrote one sentence that day: "My father is coming for Christmas." And she did her assignment. So I continued writing questions in her journal. When she answered, I wrote her longer responses, sharing information about my own experiences as a child, particularly about how I got in trouble when I misbehaved out of anger or frustration. Once I mentioned my father coming to school to "straighten me out." Tyeisha stayed after class that day and told me that my father sounded just like her father.

"Whenever my mother can't handle me anymore," Tyeisha said, "she calls my father, and he comes here to straighten me out." She smiled. "He always brings me a present. And he takes me out to dinner, and sometimes my mother comes with us."

We continued to write and talk about our families for weeks, until we finally figured out what was happening: Tyeisha's fantasy, although she knew it was impossible, was that if her mother and father spent enough time together, they would realize they still loved each other. Her father would divorce his new wife, and her mother would divorce her new husband. Her father would come back home, and their family would be the way it used to be.

"I guess that's not gonna happen," Tyeisha wrote in her journal. "So I might as well get over it. But it won't be easy because my heart is broken worse than my family is."

Unlike Tyeisha, Ivan behaved well in class, but his writing didn't match his reading scores. One of twenty-one boys enrolled in first-period remedial reading, Ivan chose not to read aloud, but his work in class clearly demonstrated good comprehension and critical thinking skills. His writing stood out because of its complexity and lack of grammatical or spelling errors. Yet he insisted that he belonged in remedial reading.

After exchanging notes in his journal for a few weeks, I visited the guidance office and asked to see Ivan's records from elementary school. From first through eighth grades, Ivan had been an honor student. He had aced all his exams and earned straight As. So why suddenly in his freshman year of high school had Ivan become a remedial reader? I posed that question in his journal. His response: "I'm just too tired, Miss J. I don't think I can do this for four more years. I think it would be better if I could just go to prison. Then I would have my own bed and I could read books. There wouldn't be people shooting guns all the time. I just don't think I can take this for four more years."

After I wiped the tears from my eyes, I realized that my task was to convince Ivan that his intelligence was his key to success, that prison was not the only alternative to his difficult life. During the following years, I learned that Ivan is not an exception. Many children today see prison as their best option. A sad statement about our society and one that all adults, especially teachers, must recognize and address.

One of Ivan's classmates, Eric, began one journal entry with the question: "How come everybody say just Say No To Drugs when they don't know what they talkin about?" Eric went on to explain that a boy who had recently been shot in his neighborhood in East

Palo Alto had not been "in the wrong place at the wrong time" as the newspapers speculated. The boy, a good student and popular classmate, had been killed during what had been described as a botched drug deal.

The day after I read Eric's journal, I asked him to stop after class and talk to me. He hesitated until I assured him that he wasn't in trouble, that I just wanted to talk. I told him I was sorry about his friend and concerned about what he had written. I said I wished he had told me sooner.

"But you said that if we used drugs you feel sorry for us, but if we sell drugs, you think we were scum."

I had said that during a class discussion about selling drugs. When one of the kids boasted that selling drugs was the easiest and fastest way to get rich, I said it was also the easiest and fastest way to make crack babies and that anybody who sold drugs was contributing to the crack baby population and therefore was scum in my book.

"Well, sometimes I say things in the heat of passion," I said. "Maybe I could have phrased my thoughts a little better. I wanted you kids to see that taking drugs changes your perception of reality, but it doesn't change your reality."

"So if I sold drugs, you wouldn't think I was scum?"

"It would depend on the circumstances," I said.

"It wasn't my idea," Eric said. "These guys in a black car with windows tinted all black be sitting by the bus stop and when we get off the bus, they pick somebody. One day they pick me. This guy comes up and puts a gun in my face and goes, 'Here's the package; here's the address; here's the money. Deliver it or you're dead.' He wasn't playing, so I delivered it. And now I'm a drug dealer. And he said if I don't keep on doing it, he'll turn me in to the cops and I'll get arrested and go to jail for being a pusher."

"And that's what happened to your friend who got killed?"

"Yeah," Eric nodded. "He said no."

I felt like crying, like screaming, like grabbing Eric and hugging him, but I knew those things would frighten him. So I covered my face with my hands for a second so that he wouldn't be able to see my expression. I didn't want him to see how much his life frightened me.

"Don't worry, Miss J," Eric said. "It's OK now."

"No, it isn't," I said. "Not if those people are making you sell drugs."

"They aren't. I fixed it."

"You went to the police?" I had thought of suggesting that, but I couldn't be sure that the police would believe Eric or overlook his participation.

"I joined a gang," Eric said. "I know you don't like gangs neither, but this isn't a bad gang. It's more like a posse. We don't be selling drugs or doing drive-bys or any of that stuff. It's just a bunch of kids, and we all chill together, and we wear the same jackets and stuff. And when we get off the bus, we hang together so those guys leave us alone. They go for the loners."

I couldn't think of a single thing to say to Eric. He stood looking at me for a few seconds, then patted my shoulder.

"It's all right, Miss J. Sometimes you gotta do what you gotta do."

One of these days, I gotta get that Ph.D.

4

Memo to the Boss

To: School Administrators

From: The Queen of Education

Subject: The Royal Sixteen

The queen most respectfully forwards the following sixteen suggestions to administrators who wish to retain the bright and shining
new teachers on their staffs. Because more than 25 percent of new
teachers quit within the first three years of service, it is paramount
that we pay attention to them immediately, while we still may.

1. Make Them Effective Managers

Some teachers instinctively know how to gain control of a classroom, but most new teachers find this to be their greatest problem
and the primary reason they throw in the chalk and walk away
from our schools. Classroom management is part of every teacher-
training program today. Unfortunately, many of the techniques and
theories presented during teaching-training courses simply do not
work when applied to real children—especially techniques that
focus on punitive discipline. Although some of these methods may
reduce the amount of noise and movement in a room, they don't
foster a good rapport between student and teacher; and many of
them backfire so badly that they end up creating more serious discipline problems.

Creating a list of rules and consequences does not automatically result in good behavior. Threats and punishment create tension, frustration, and anger in the classroom; and both students and teachers go on guard, waiting for the next confrontation to occur. But when an atmosphere of sincere mutual respect exists, the dynamic shifts and students willingly control their behavior—because they want to, not because they are afraid of being punished. The key to classroom control is forging a bond between teacher and student. Sadly, many new teachers march into the classroom, armed with a rule book, a pad of detention slips, and a determination to impose order. Before they even learn their students' names, those teachers find themselves standing on one side of a huge chasm, shouting at the nameless students who stare at them from the other side.

Ask your staff to recommend some good books and videos on classroom management. Have these on hand for new teachers. At the start of the school year, remind your new teachers that effective classroom management consists of some basic principles:

Prevention. Effective teachers do not hide behind their desks or lecterns. They move about the room, make eye contact, and use body language to warn potential troublemakers that they are entering the danger zone.

Respect. Good classroom managers make students responsible for their own behavior. They correct students in order to help them make better choices, not to punish them. They use referrals to the principal, parent phone calls, detention, and so on only as a last resort. They offer students their sincere respect—and they get back what they give.

Options. Effective teachers don't back students against the wall. They allow students to survive a confrontation without losing face. And they allow students to choose one of three options: change the present behavior, take a time-out to consider the situation, or continue the unacceptable behavior and suffer the consequences that the school's disciplinary code outlines.

2. Lighten the Load

Assign new teachers the minimum number of different subjects to teach, instead of the maximum in an effort to please the veteran teachers on your staff. The vets are more prepared, more experienced, and much more likely to complain no matter how many different class preparations you assign them. Some experienced teachers enjoy nothing more than complaining about how much harder than everybody else they work. Assigning them more preps will provide them with welcome fuel for their lunchroom rants and tirades. Your compassionate veteran teachers will understand that their extra effort will help new teachers build the teaching muscles they will need to handle those heavier loads.

Your new teachers will need time to create classroom environments that fit their teaching styles. If teachers at your school must move from room to room or from building to building during the school day, new teachers should be last on the list of those required to trot about, toting their teaching tools. They have enough to juggle without having to worry about lugging their lessons from here to eternity.

Whenever possible, allow new teachers to continue teaching the same subjects and grade levels the following year (and for a third or fourth). This will enable them to become experts in one area and to develop a professional portfolio of assignments. Their confidence and morale will increase as they enter their second year and they will be happier, more effective teachers.

3. Show Them How It's Done

Encourage new teachers to visit and observe the classrooms of successful teachers, not just teachers in their own subject area. An English newbie can learn much from watching a dynamic biology instructor, just as a social studies teacher may pick up some good tips from a math whiz. Observing a master teacher in action for a few hours is worth a semester of sitting in a college classroom reading about classroom management.

If a new teacher seems to be struggling with lesson presentation, discipline, leadership, or student motivation, volunteer to fill in once a week yourself so that your new teacher can go observe another staff member who excels in the problem area. By acting as a teacher substitute, you will accomplish several worthwhile goals: you will provide your new teacher with invaluable training; you will give recognition to the successful experienced teacher; you will give students a chance to brag to their friends that the principal taught their class; and you will develop a better rapport and understanding of the students in your school. Not bad for an hour's work.

4. Limit Extracurricular Assignments

Instead of requiring that all teachers sign up to sponsor a club or event, allow new teachers the option of volunteering only if they feel confident that they have a handle on their professional duties. Be aware that many newbies believe they must volunteer for assignments in order to earn good evaluations; make sure that they understand your evaluations will be based on their teaching. At the start of the year, idealistic new teachers may feel capable of taking on any number of assignments; but by Christmastime many of them will be lagging behind the pack. Spring break will find them exhausted and stretched so thin that they are in danger of disappearing the moment the school year ends.

Many new teachers are drafted, coerced, or volunteered into acting as coaches, club sponsors, yearbook editors, team chaperons, or detention monitors when they are struggling already to keep up with their grading and class assignments. Allow them a year or two of basic teaching duty before you pile on more responsibilities. What may take a veteran teacher thirty minutes to accomplish may take a new teacher several hours—simply because the new teacher is unfamiliar with the planning, processes, and procedures required.

If you simply must assign new teachers to extra duties, try to offer assignments that require the least amount of time and effort, such as being chaperons for senior prom or homecoming. Or let them monitor Saturday school or other programs that allow them to receive payment for working overtime.

5. Halve Your Staff Development

For every staff development or in-service day, allow teachers to spend half the day collaborating with each other or working in their own classrooms. New teachers desperately seek more time to work without interruption, and you will do them a great service if you can provide this time. Many of your veteran teachers also need this prep time in order to remain effective. Veteran teachers who have all their ducks in a row can circulate and assist the newer teachers. Your vets can offer advice based on their years of experience, but they may also learn new, creative approaches from the new teachers.

Take excruciating care to ensure that the staff development programs you offer address your faculty's real concerns. The most dynamic speaker will meet with yawns and indifference if his or her focus is one of the current hot buzzwords that isn't in your teachers' working vocabulary. And after the lectures and presentations, let your local experts—your teachers—strut their stuff. Schedule time for them to talk to each other, to compare and share their successes and failures, their problems and solutions. Group your teachers by subject or grade level or let them mingle and talk to each other without a structured agenda. This will allow new teachers to form friendships among the staff, which is an important aspect of a profession in which people work in isolation from their peers. For a new teacher to hear that she or he is not the Lone Ranger when it comes to discipline problems can do much to foster confidence.

6. Cover Their Backs (and Backsides)

Support your new teachers. Do not hang them out to dry. Do not disregard their concerns. If they have problems with students or parents or guardians, provide whatever support you can. Do not embarrass or belittle the new teacher in front of anybody, especially students or other staff members. If a conflict occurs in your presence, back your teacher unless you have good reason to believe he or she is in the wrong. Then investigate and make your decision based on full knowledge. If a teacher asks you for help in disciplining students, provide that help. Remember that new teachers would not consult you if they felt capable of handling situations on their own.

Of course, new teachers are going to make mistakes. Unless you have led a completely immaculate error-free life, it would behoove you to ponder your own past, which may inspire you to provide moral and professional support to your teachers. If they make mistakes repeatedly, correct them in private and provide some resource for them to receive additional training in the area that needs attention, perhaps classroom management, conflict resolution, positive discipline, or leadership.

Make sure your new teachers are aware of particularly important political and legal situations in your community. Every community has a distinctive mix of political and religious persuasions, with subjects of particular interest to local residents. In some districts, for example, teaching evolution is a hotly contested danger zone and one that a new science teacher may have difficulty navigating without some guidance from administration. High rates of domestic violence, parental apathy or overinvolvement, drug abuse, gang activity, teen pregnancy, or homelessness in your school district may also affect the way teachers should approach students and parents. Prepare your teachers by providing an accurate and complete assessment of your community. You won't scare your new teachers away by preparing them for difficult situations; if they were fainthearted, they would not have become teachers in the first place. By giving them the "straight skinny," you may help them avoid getting caught off guard and making mistakes from which it may be difficult or impossible to recover.

7. Provide Multiple Mentors

Make sure that every new teacher on your staff has at least three mentors available for consultation. Do not limit mentors to senior staff, but also assign those juniors who appear to be natural teachers. Encourage two or more new teachers to form a team, which may require that they switch or merge classes or develop cross-curriculum assignments. Keep an eye out for new teachers who always seem to be alone. Perhaps they enjoy the solitude of lunching solo after teaching all morning, but perhaps they feel intimidated or unwelcome in the teachers' lunchroom. If your new teachers' only introduction to the other teachers was a brief welcome to all the newcomers, accompanied by stares and applause from the rest of the faculty and staff, then it's time to make some personal introductions.

Until you have a good idea of who would make a good match among your teachers, don't assign permanent mentors. Provide a checklist and ask senior staff members to escort your new teachers around your campus, pointing out key locations such as textbook supply, staff restrooms, department offices, the copy center, the media arts room, the computer lab, lounges, and the teachers' lunchroom. Once you have time to discover your new teachers' unique personalities, you will be able to assign permanent mentors who are likely to provide a true service.

Beware the overeager volunteer. Some veteran staff members may volunteer to serve as mentors simply because they want to recruit the newbies to join their side of political, professional, or personal skirmishes at your school. Make sure that the mentors you assign are effective teachers who enjoy the respect of peers and students alike. You may do your new teachers a huge disservice by assigning them mentors who are burned out, bitter, or counting the days until they can retire.

Reach out to your community for mentors. Retired educators and administrators in your community may be delighted to serve as mentors. Consider asking instructors at local colleges and universities who enjoy reputations as excellent educators. Invite those mentors who are not district employees to attend your school's staff meetings, and encourage them to visit your teachers in their classrooms.

8. Keep Them Connected

If your classrooms do not have internal phone lines, make sure that new teachers are assigned to classrooms with two-way intercoms so that they can contact the office when they need guidance or emergency assistance. If phones or intercoms are not available, then provide a walkie-talkie or beeper. Don't leave your new teachers stranded without a way to call for backup.

Encourage the parent connection. Parental support and participation is key to student success. Provide suggestions, guidance, and moral support for new teachers as they initiate and maintain contact with parents and guardians. Support them if they encounter difficulties. Let parents know that you value your teachers and stand behind them (unless you have a very good reason not to).

Provide a private area where teachers have access to an outside telephone line for calling parents. Because new teachers tend to work longer hours, they need to be able to make telephone calls from the school premises during early morning, after-school, and evening hours. If necessary, provide teachers a shared cell phone, a detailed phone log, and a schedule that allows every teacher specific times to use the phone.

9. Visit Your Fledglings

Pay frequent visits to new teachers' classrooms—not to criticize them or evaluate them but to offer moral support and guidance when needed. Observe them often so that they will not panic when you do show up for an official evaluation. (Please do not be one of those pseudoadministrators who never visit classrooms yet somehow magically create the evaluations the district office requires. Inexperienced teachers need real evaluations if they are to become excellent experienced teachers.)

Make sure that your teachers feel comfortable asking for advice, instead of fearing that they will lose their jobs or receive poor evaluations if they admit they have problems. Of course, they will have problems. But you can do much to alleviate those problems by being available and accessible to them. Also, as you visit the classrooms of new teachers and chat with them in front of students, students will get the message that you and your teachers are playing on the same team. This can foster better behavior and pride among students.

If a new teacher has a particularly troublesome group of students, offer to work out some kind of deal with the students wherein you challenge them to complete a difficult project or achieve a minimum average grade in return for a special reward that you will pay for out of your own pocket (a pizza party, a movie rental, a stand-up comic, or magician to visit their room). Students find it immensely thrilling to get something free from the principal. In addition to helping the teacher by motivating students, you will have the opportunity to build a better rapport with those students who are most likely to be referred to your office by their teachers.

10. Provide Electronic Grading

You can eliminate hours of frustration and save many more hours of work time by providing computer software that enables electronic-gradebooks for your teachers. Equally important, however, is providing teachers training in setting up the computerized grading program and allowing them time to enter the required data. Just entering the names and student numbers for one class of twenty-five students into a computerized grade book can take an hour. Then teachers must break assignments down into different units or topics. For each subject the teacher must decide how much weight each assignment and exam will carry. Then the teacher has to create columns and type in the name of each assignment, quiz, and test. Eventually, all this input will enable the teacher to print out individual student progress reports, average test scores for a specific class, award extra credit, and calculate grades at lightning speeds, but setting up the files at the beginning can be a slow and tedious process. At the start of the year when students add, drop, and shift from class to class, teachers must spend more time at the keyboard to stay up-to-date.

If your staff includes a computer whiz in the guidance department, you may be able to provide a master disk with names, student numbers, phone numbers, and parent or guardian information for the students on your new teachers' roll sheets. Or perhaps you could provide a computer-competent student assistant, a veteran teacher, or a support technician to help the newbies learn how to manipulate the grading program.

In addition to making life easier for new teachers, electronic-gradebook programs can also motivate students. Many children enjoy having a printed record of their progress. Periodic reports provide them with visual proof that they are moving toward their goals; and status reports can prevent shock, trauma, and arguments about grades for both students and their parents. When a student's grade starts to slump, the teacher can call the student aside, pull up the student's existing grades, and enter data to demonstrate how easily his or her grade could jump one letter. Students often fail to understand how one or two missing assignments can lower their overall grade. Electronic grade reports can capture the attention of today's computer-savvy students, who may not hear or heed warnings or lectures.

11. Provide Sample Lesson Plans

Yes, new teachers should know how to create lesson plans. Most of them do, but creating a lesson plan to meet the requirements of an education course is like producing a piece of cake from a boxed mix. Creating a viable lesson plan based on unfamiliar textbooks; incorporating district and state curriculum guidelines and benchmarks; including mandatory tests as well as those the teacher initiates; avoiding conflicts with field trips, sporting events, homecoming, prom, picture day, open house, staff development days, and schoolwide exams—now, that's a seven-course gourmet dinner made from scratch.

You can do much to foster efficient time management, appropriate lessons, peace of mind, and high morale among your inexperienced staff members by providing sample lesson plans and curriculum outlines prepared by veteran teachers. Provide a variety of different styles so that your new teachers realize that there isn't one correct way to design and present information on any subject; let them see that all good lesson plans share some basics.

Assure new teachers that you understand they may occasionally have to depart from their lesson outlines, because students quite often surprise teachers by taking more or less time than expected to complete a unit. Many new teachers worry that if they aren't doing exactly what they said they would when they said they would, you will lose faith in them and believe they are untrustworthy. If a new teacher repeatedly has problems sticking to lesson plans, encourage that teacher to spend some time reviewing lesson plans of senior teachers on the staff and rereading district curriculum guidelines, which often offer broad suggestions for materials to cover in a quarter or semester.

12. Pay Them

If your school has a budget for task forces or summer training programs, pay your new teachers to participate in those projects so that they won't have to teach summer school in order to eat. Many new teachers sign up to teach summer school without realizing that they need an emotional and mental vacation from teaching in order to avoid burning out when the new school year begins. Those new teachers who staunchly believe they are immune to burnout are those who are most likely to spend inordinate amounts of time and energy, ending up exhausted before Christmas vacation.

Give teachers free passes to school athletic events. This will not only boost their budgets but will encourage them to support their students and interact with them outside of academics. A chat in the bleachers or a wave across the football field can do more to cement the bond between student and teacher than can any number of conversations in the classroom.

Encourage local merchants to give discounts to teachers. A dollar off dinner, a discount on office supplies, and free checking at the bank may save your impoverished new teachers from another night of instant noodle soup.

13. Feed Them

Whenever possible, provide nutritious meals for new teachers. Not coffee, doughnuts, and pastries—diabetes and obesity are rampant in our schools. Offer bottled water and caffeine-free iced tea. Provide platters of fresh raw vegetables with dips and olives, bowls of pretzels and baked chips, salads, whole-grain crackers and low-fat cheeses, sandwiches, yogurt—the kinds of foods that feed the brain and foster thought. You will find that teachers who are hungry (and most new teachers are hungry all the time) are less efficient and productive than are those whose stomachs are well satisfied.

P.S. You will earn high marks from your teachers if you arrange for the vending machine in the teacher's lounge to carry a variety of healthy alternatives to chips and candy, so that teachers who work late or early can grab a snack that won't ruin their health or their ability to concentrate.

14. Teach Portfolio Design

Experienced teachers know that assignments requiring students to work independently over a period of days or weeks to produce an individual portfolio offer the best way to assess student learning, allow for vastly different rates of learning, permit the teacher to work closely with students who need more help, foster creativity and motivation, and provide the opportunity for students to practice time management and goal setting along with new academic skills. But new teachers usually feel overwhelmed at the mere thought of portfolio assignments. Many variables and questions come to mind: How do I design a portfolio? How long should it be? How much time should students have to complete the project? Which sections should I grade most heavily? How should I present the assignment to the students? How much weight should I give to the portfolio grade? What if good students fail to complete the project—should they fail the course or receive a lower grade than what they would have earned? How much noise and confusion is acceptable during class time? How do I monitor thirty or more individual workers? What about students who can't seem to work without external motivation? What if the whole class seems to be floundering?

You can answer these questions and inspire your staff to tap into their own creative intelligences by providing instruction in portfolio design and implementation. Provide sample portfolios that students at your school have submitted. (If nobody at your school uses portfolios, look for good examples online or in education textbooks.) Invite teachers to share their best projects. Suggest different approaches to grading the portfolios. Ask for volunteers who will help new teachers implement their first portfolio assignment by visiting the classroom, if possible, or meeting regularly to discuss points of concern.

15. Avoid Stacking the Deck

I know administrators are busy and don't need one more thing to take up their time just as the school year begins. But you will save yourself and your new teachers many hours of aggravation later on if you take a few minutes to review your new teachers' rosters before classes start. Check to make sure that not all the bad apples are in your newbies' classrooms. Every school has a handful (some have many hands full, unfortunately) of truly troubled students who require superhuman patience and energy from their teachers. Those troubled students often end up, by accident or design, in the classrooms of new teachers who are not equipped to deal with them. And this is not a case in which on-the-job training will make a better teacher. Some newbies may rise to the challenge, but most will shrink or shriek—and nobody wins. The student spends too much time in detention (or in your office); the new teacher loses more confidence and sleep than he or she can afford to lose; and your counseling and disciplinary staff have to scramble to pick up the pieces after your new teacher cracks.

No, you can't protect your new teachers from difficult students (and parents). But you can make sure that your new teachers are not stuck with all the students that nobody else has been able to teach or all the demanding parents that other teachers have failed to please in the past. A quick check of all the class rosters for your English department, for example, will give you an idea of whether the deck is stacked against your newbies. If it is, please unstack it.

16. Say Thank You, Thank You, Thank You

Most teachers are willing to teach in spite of more lucrative opportunities—they aren't in it for the money. They teach because it is the most frustrating, difficult, challenging, and satisfying work in the world. Make sure your teachers know that you know they are special people. At least once each semester, stop each teacher in the hallways and thank him or her for teaching. Stop the new teachers twice. Tell them you realize teaching is a challenging and difficult profession, in spite of its many rewards, and that you appreciate their willingness to work on behalf of young people. Shake their hands. Thank them on the intercom. Thank them in the school newsletter. Thank them at staff meetings. Thank them especially after open house and parents' day. Thank them with words, food, books, money, prizes, with discounts at local banks, restaurants, and shops. In the case of teachers, the trite is true: you cannot thank them enough.

5

Down with Detention

Using detention as a catchall cure for student misbehaviors is like using one medicine for every physical ailment. We would not expect a single prescription medication to cure a cold, flu, broken bone, ulcer, headache, heart attack, and cancer—yet we expect one punishment to address tardiness, aggression, bullying, emotional illness, inattention, fear, anger, laziness, excessive talking, defiance, childish exuberance, alcoholism, daydreaming, forgetfulness, profanity, truancy, immaturity, drug abuse, cheating, lying, stealing, and extortion among schoolchildren.

Sentencing students to detention creates more problems than it solves, but still most public schools continue the practice. At one high school where I taught freshman English, I was directed to send all tardy students to detention after the first-period bell, regardless of the reason for their tardiness. When I questioned the procedure, the instructional vice principal informed me that I had to conform to the policy that the freshman teachers had created if I expected them to consider me a team player.

After considerable thought I decided that educating my students and maintaining my ethics took priority over my popularity among my peers. I did not send tardy students to detention but required them to come in during lunchtime and make up the time they had missed.

"You need to be here on time," I explained to my students. "But I realize that life sometimes makes punctuality difficult. Since we want you to act like young adults in this school, I am going to treat you like young adults. If you're late for work or for a college class, you don't blow it off and go home. You get there as fast as you can and quietly get to work without disturbing other people. When the supervisor isn't busy, you offer your excuse and apology. That's what I want you to do here."

My students responded to my policy by making a real effort to arrive on time. Those who were tardy made up the time without complaints, and their behavior and motivation improved as well because they understood that I was honestly trying to help them succeed in school and prepare for life after graduation.

At the end of the first quarter of that school semester, the freshman teachers met to review a spreadsheet showing the failure rates for each of our classes. My failure rate of 7 percent was the only single-digit rate on the sheet. More than half of the teachers had failure rates of 25 percent or higher.

"These kids don't care," said the math teacher whose classroom was next door to mine. I bit my tongue to prevent myself from pointing out that although he was the freshman team leader, he sent more students to detention than did any of the other teachers.

During our discussion with the vice principal about methods to increase our students' grades and motivation, I couldn't keep quiet. I said that I believed the detention policy for tardies was extreme and that it resulted in lower grades and many more discipline problems.

"I think I could make a list right now of students, especially boys, who are being sent to detention frequently. Their behavior is going downhill along with their grades; and I think that by the time these students are juniors, they will be failing most of their classes and will be at high risk of dropping out. If they don't drop out, they'll go into an alternative school, juvenile detention, or some kind of dropout prevention program. I'd like to develop an alternate strategy for dealing with these students, one that addresses specific behavior issues and one that doesn't punish them academically."

After about sixty seconds of dead silence, the vice principal closed her agenda book and said, "I don't think that will be necessary."

The following week, when the tardy bell rang, the math teacher stood outside my door, turning students away.

"What are you doing?" I asked.

"Sending these kids to detention where they belong," the math teacher said.

"But they're my students," I argued. "I should be the one to deal with them."

"We have to have consistency among the freshman teachers," the math teacher explained. "If we don't, the kids will take advantage."

I will spare you the gory details. At the end of the semester, I resigned my job at that school. I wrestled with the decision for many nights, but I simply couldn't bring myself to participate in such a punitive system. I couldn't pretend to believe the system was acceptable, and I couldn't ignore the system without creating a backlash of anger and retaliation against my students or myself.

I wish I could say that school was unusual, but it wasn't. At another high school, teachers were instructed to lock the doors to their classroom one second after the final bell rang to indicate the start of each class period—even if students were racing down the corridors toward their classrooms. As tardy students pounded on the doors to the closed classrooms, security guards rounded up students and escorted them to the detention center, where they were required to perform word search games and other elementary worksheets but not permitted to complete classroom assignments. When I took a folder filled with assignments to the detention center and asked the monitor to give it to one of my students, the monitor told me that students weren't allowed to do classwork because they were being punished.

"But that doesn't address the issue of tardiness," I argued.

"I don't make the rules," the monitor said, "but I have to follow them."

I didn't argue with the monitor. Instead, I asked questions of various staff members and learned that the monitor was not a certificated teacher or classroom aide. The following day, after the roundup of the usual suspects, I went to the detention center each period with a slip of paper on which I had written the names of the students missing from my class. When the monitor answered the door, I handed him the paper and said, "I am Miss Johnson, and I need these students, if they are here."

The monitor would glance at the note, check his log book, and read off the names of my students. I would nod curtly at the monitor and sternly advise the students to "listen up and follow me." The students complied, looking bewildered and wary.

As the first group of rescued students approached my classroom, one of the students cleared his throat and asked, "What's up, Miss J?"

"I am responsible for your academic education, your safety, and your well-being during this class period. I didn't send you to detention. If you acted up in somebody else's class, then you work it out with that teacher. And if you were there for just being tardy, then we'll work on that. But if I were you, I'd keep this conversation to myself."

"That's cool," the boy said.

"I'm not trying to be cool," I explained. "I'm trying to be reasonable. What were you doing in detention?"

"My dad drives me to school," the boy said, "and he always be running a little bit late in the mornings."

"And doesn't that cause problems for him at work?" I asked.

"Nope." The boy shrugged. "He's a contractor, so he doesn't have to be on site as soon as the work crew. He just has to show up and supervise."

"Well, I'm the contractor in my classroom," I said, "and you're in the work crew. So you have to show up on time."

"Hey," the kid held out both hands, palms up. "What am I supposed to do? We already had two parent conferences, and my dad says he'll make sure I'm here on time, but he keeps on being late. It's not my fault."

"Yes, it is," I said. "You aren't a little kid. You're a young man. If your dad can't get you here on time, you need to arrange other transportation. Hitch a ride with a friend, walk, jog, ride your bike, take the city bus, ride your skateboard. But you need to figure out how to get here on time. Or else I'm going to meet you here on Saturday mornings to make up the time and work you missed from my class, and I'm not as charming on weekends as I am during the week."

"Can you do that?" the kid asked.

"If you want to find out, you just keep coming to school late."

"That's messed up," the kid said.

"No, it isn't," I said. "It's logical and reasonable. Your behavior is hurting your grades, and I want you to be a successful student. So I am trying to help you change the behavior that prevents you from being successful. Can you explain to me how that is 'messed up'?"

"I guess it isn't," he said.

I turned to the two girls who were straggling behind us, hoping to become invisible. "How about you two? Why were you in detention?"

"We had to go to the restroom," one of the girls said.

I recalled that the same two girls had been in detention the previous week for the same reason.

"You didn't have time to go before the bell? Or maybe you were busy talking to your friends? Or your boyfriends?"

The girls exchanged glances, then both became very interested in their shoes.

"Come on," I said. "I'm not going to yell at you. I'm trying to help you solve this problem."

One of the girls bit her lip and squinted at me. The other one refused to make eye contact.

"I'm not going to send you to the office or call your parents or punish you. I'm trying to help you be successful students."

After a few seconds, the girl who had squinted at me glanced at the boy. "It's personal," she whispered.

"Well, you think about it, and I'll see you after class."

After class the girls explained that they rushed to eat breakfast at 6:30 before catching the bus for the half-hour trip to school. By the time they arrived on campus, they both needed to use the restroom, and they couldn't wait until after first period. So they waited until the warning bell rang and then tried to hurry and use the restroom before the final bell. Usually, they missed the bell by less than a minute.

"If you ride the bus, then you have time to use the restroom before first period," I said. "Unless the bus is late, and that doesn't happen often. So I'm not buying your excuse. But I would really like to help you. So why not tell me the truth?"

I leaned against the wall and started to cross my arms over my chest, a typical waiting-for-an-answer posture. Then I remembered a recent article I'd read on body language. Instead of leaning back, I made myself stand in exactly the same posture as the two girls. I shifted my weight to one leg and stood with my hands behind my back, looking at the ground.

After a long silence, the smaller girl said, "Well, there's these older girls. Seniors."

"Yeah, but most of them flunked a couple times," added her friend. "So they're pretty old. And they're kinda tough."

"Sometimes they shove people or pull their hair," said the small girl. "And sometimes they smoke and . . ."

She paused when the taller girl coughed softly. "And, um, other stuff."

"OK," I said. "So why don't you use a different bathroom?"

"The ones in the gym are locked until first period, and the ones in C Hall is even worse than the one near your room. Some kids even have sex in there. I'm not lying."

Sadly, I knew she wasn't. I told them to come and get me in the mornings when they arrived, and I would escort them to the restroom until we found another solution.

"If I'm not here, you go to the office and ask the vice principal's secretary to send security to check the restroom."

Both girls looked stricken. "They'll kill us for telling on them."

"I'll talk to the secretary and make sure she doesn't mention your names, so that those girls won't know you told me about them."

They still looked unconvinced.

"Trust me," I said. "Nobody will know. And if you walk into the restroom and those girls are there, just turn around and walk out. If they follow you, run and scream your heads off."

They both giggled. And they agreed to try my plan. That afternoon I spoke to one of the security guards who frequently patrolled the hallway near my classroom. He said he usually concentrated on the bus zone in the mornings because that's where most problems occurred, but that he would go with me to check the restroom where the girls were having trouble. We never caught them in the act of doing anything illegal, but within a couple of weeks, the girls who had been lurking in the restrooms decided to move their social salon elsewhere, leaving the rooms free for students who needed to use them.

Had I not intervened in this situation, the two girls—and probably many other students—would have continued being sent to detention for being tardy because they lacked the problem-solving skills needed to find a solution. In addition to wasting the students' time, the situation would have resulted in wasted effort on behalf of their first-period teacher, pointless paperwork passed between the detention monitor and the office, parent conferences after the fifth referral, and possibly more severe punishments. And it is very likely that those two girls would have learned to hate school.

Put Yourself in Their Shoes

Imagine that you overslept one day and arrived at work late. Or you forgot to bring the PowerPoint presentation that you and your coworkers were scheduled to present to an important client. Perhaps you made a serious mistake on the job: you got involved in a heated argument with a coworker; you argued with your boss when she assigned you a menial chore; you took a much-needed mental health day and bumped into your supervisor at the golf course.

Now imagine that when you report to work the day after your tardiness, forgetfulness, temper tantrum, or fake illness, your supervisor sends you to the human resources office, where someone tells you that you must sit in an empty conference room for an hour or a day or after work. You must sit in the empty room, staring at the walls while your fellow workers receive valuable training that they will need in order to perform important work functions in the future. You will not be permitted to make up the training, but your supervisor may give you a quick summary when you return to work. You will be expected to be able to perform the newly required tasks as effectively as your fellow employees. If you can't learn the skills your coworkers learned while you were absent, you risk being demoted, censured, or fired.

Or imagine that instead of being sent to sit in a conference room, you are sent home for the day without pay. You will miss the important training and will not receive any kind of follow-up. Your boss will, however, expect you to figure out how to do the tasks that your fellow workers learned to do during your absence if you expect to be paid or promoted.

These scenarios sound unreasonable, don't they? They are illogical. They don't address your particular problem, and they certainly don't motivate you to do your best work for your company. They may motivate you to dust off your résumé and look for another job.

Yet these same absurd approaches to behavior modification are in use at most public schools. In spite of the illogic of the approach and the repeated failure to achieve the desired goal, most schools still maintain a variation of the standard detention or in-school suspension (ISS) program, which does not include an effective behavior modification component or a humane approach.

Educators don't really believe that students who are disciplined through detention or ISS will emerge with improved attitudes toward school, a sincere desire to behave better, new motivation to excel academically, or a burning desire to cooperate with teachers. Anybody who has completed even an elementary course in psychology knows that expecting to change children's behavior and attitudes by shutting them away and ignoring them is ridiculous. Although removing children from the group is a good start, in addition to the time-out, children must be taught to analyze their own behavior and to figure out what made them misbehave in the first place. Then they must be required to take responsibility for their behavior and taught how to make better choices. Detention and ISS don't accomplish any goal, except to remove children from the group.

Educators use detention and ISS to make their own lives easier. Their primary motive is to remove troubling children from classrooms, regardless of the reason for the trouble or the academic consequence for those students. If detention and ISS programs did work, they would phase themselves out of existence by changing student behavior. Instead, they continue to grow until they become so large and unwieldy that districts must adopt other solutions— alternative schools, at-risk programs, parenting programs, behavior modification classes, teen court, peer counseling, and mentor programs, among others. These new solutions do what schools should have done in the first place: they find out why a particular behavior occurred and work with the student to change the behavior. Schools could save time, money, and considerable heartache by replacing detention programs with alternate solutions.

I believe that if we kept track of students who are sent to detention or ISS frequently during fifth through ninth grades, we would find that those are the same students who drop out of school or become serious behavior problems in senior high school. The downward spiral begins when a student is assigned detention for being tardy, mouthy, uncooperative, or unable or unwilling to complete homework and assignments. Most likely, this student is not a scholar but one who reads at or below grade level. Now she misses valuable instruction time that she cannot make up, misses classroom exercises and discussion, and falls further behind the class. Even if she is allowed to make up missed assignments, chances are that she will not make them up or will copy them or will do a poor job. The teacher now has the added stress of trying to catch the student up (if the teacher is inclined to do so, which may not be the case if the teacher and student have a personality conflict). The student perceives the teacher's frustration as dislike, and she withdraws or rebels. And so the problem isn't solved—it is compounded. Now the student is scared, angry, or confused (probably all three) and either gives up on learning the missed work or decides to pay back the teacher, which will result in further punishment. The student earns a poor grade and misses important skills and knowledge that will be required in future classes. Logically, the student decides that if the school doesn't care about her, then she doesn't care about school.

Wouldn't it make more sense to address the actual behaviors that result in students being sent to detention?

Many problems in school stem from a student's inability to do the assigned work or from boredom because the student finds the work too easy. In my own experience, the worst behavior comes from the worst and best readers. Students who are repeatedly uncooperative or unmotivated should take a diagnostic reading exam to assess their reading level and comprehension skills.

Students who cannot read well struggle in nearly every class. Regardless of their intelligence, they cannot solve math problems if they cannot read and understand the problems. Likewise, they cannot grasp a scientific concept if they can't comprehend the explanation. And unlike adults, who have many options when placed in a position where they are ill prepared to perform, students rarely have viable options. Many schools have only one or two math or science classes per grade level, so changing instructors isn't an option. Required courses must be taken at specific times, regardless of the students' varying stages of intellectual development. So students feel stuck, and often they are.

Poor readers begin to fall behind during the second or third grade. Each year they fall further behind; and the further they fall, the less confidence they have when the next school year begins. By the time they reach junior high school, poor readers believe they are stupid, lazy, unteachable, and destined for failure. If they don't get help, most of them will find a way to be removed from classes so that they don't have to sit for hours on end, feeling embarrassed and hopeless. They much prefer to be sent to the office or detention where no one will expect them to read out loud or decipher difficult textbooks. And unfortunately, the so-called tough kids earn more respect among their peers than do the special ed kids. Sadly, many poor readers believe their only choice is to be labeled bad or dumb.

Struggling students need extensive programs for remedial reading (and should earn credits for this instruction). They should be routinely tested for scotopic sensitivity (see Chapter Nine), perceptual differences, and learning styles. Instead of blaming the child, we would do better to spend our efforts and dollars determining why a child can't read and finding a way to teach that child.

Students who act out in class because they are bored silly need to be intellectually challenged, either by independent assignments in the regular classroom or enrollment in gifted or accelerated classes. They may also benefit from performing peer tutoring or taking self-paced computerized instruction in the school library. Mature students may be excused from school to attend college classes on-line or at a local university.

Some people would argue that reading assessments are routine at every school. Extra testing and instruction, along with the other options I have suggested, would cost too much money. I would argue that if you tabulate the costs of administration (referrals, phone calls, letters, special ed evaluations, Individual Education Plans, police and social services representatives, parent conferences, probation officers, and parole officers) and the vast amount of time, energy, and paper that teachers and administrators spend on punitive discipline, you would find that detention is inordinately expensive. Add the cost of dropout prevention programs and programs for at-risk youth, and the price keeps rising. Teaching kids to read in school instead of jail is cheaper and more humane.

According to the U.S. Department of Education and the U.S. Bureau of Justice, 70 percent of prison inmates are functionally illiterate and 85 percent of juvenile offenders have reading problems.[1] Perhaps if those inmates had learned to read properly as children, they would have chosen other options than the behavior that resulted in their imprisonment.

Respect Works Both Ways—and It Does Work!

Although it would be impossible to list the many misbehaviors that may occur and prescribe a solution to each problem, it is possible to develop a consistent and effective approach to discipline that will address most problems. We can reduce or even eliminate discipline problems if we follow the example of natural teachers, those who seem not to have any problem maintaining order, even among students who are unruly in other classrooms.

I am not the best teacher in the world. I know that. But I am a very good teacher, according to the toughest critics in the world— students. I have always found it difficult to articulate my classroom management methods. Perhaps my background as a psychology major and military journalist helped. It certainly taught me much about human nature and the elements of leadership. But I believe it was my students who taught me how to teach. When I began teaching, I was assigned to a class of supposedly unteachable high school freshmen. Within a week those students and I had developed such a good rapport that we all enjoyed coming to class. When people asked me how I did it, I shrugged my shoulders.

"It's simple," I would say. "You just have to respect them and listen to them."

At the time I didn't understand why other teachers would sigh and shake their heads, as though I were intentionally being obtuse. When they insisted that they did respect their students, I secretly wondered whether they were just pretending. Otherwise, why wouldn't their students respond as mine had? After years of obser-

---

[1]U.S. Department of Education, National Adult Literacy Survey, 1993. *Literacy Behind Prison Walls*, U.S. Government Printing Office document #065-000-00716-9, 1994.

vation, conversation, and research, I have finally learned how to articulate my approach:

1. I like my students, although I may not always like what they do. I am able to separate the child from the behavior.

2. I passionately believe in the importance of the material I teach, and I communicate that passion to my students.

3. I believe that every student has the right to be treated with basic dignity and respect, and I communicate that belief frequently.

4. I believe it is far more important to be an A person than to be an A student. Grades can be improved; a rotten personality can ruin your life.

5. I am aware that I make mistakes. When I make them in the classroom, I apologize either when it happens or at the next opportunity.

6. I model the behavior I want my students to exhibit, especially when dealing with conflicts.

7. I expect my students to be responsible for their behavior, and I do not allow them to make me or anybody else responsible.

8. I give students a graceful way to back down when they have created a conflict. If they can choose to behave without losing face, they are much more likely to behave.

9. I thank them every day for their good behavior because I honestly appreciate it.

10. When I have students who behave regularly, I call their parents or guardians and thank them, because I know well-behaved children did not learn to behave by accident.

From the very first moment we enter the classroom, I really look at my students. I see them as human beings. I make eye contact with each student individually many times during a class period. Those students who are prone to misbehavior get the first eye contact, and that eye contact may last one or two seconds longer, but they don't receive more attention (which they perceive as a reward for acting out). I notice their hair styles, makeup, clothing, facial hair, acne, piercing, interactions and refusal to interact with other students, and other body language. Specifically, I am alert for any body language that might indicate trouble—staring, heavy breathing, teeth clenching, shifting in their seats, requests to change seating assignments, and so on. If I suspect that two or more students may be irritating each other, I rearrange their seats so that they cannot easily make eye contact. Then I watch to see which one of them initiates trouble. That's who I talk to first.

When I ask a student to change his or her seat, I always phrase this as a request and not an order. And I preface my request with this statement: "My goal is for you to be a successful student. I don't see that happening right now. I think you would be more successful if you changed your seat." Then I wait for a response. If the student is being picked on, he or she will gladly move. If the student argues that he or she doesn't want to move, then I say, "Fine. If you think you can be successful in this seat, then I will respect your judgment. But if I find that you disrupt my teaching or somebody else's learning again, then I will have to insist that you move and there won't be any argument. All right?"

If the student agrees, then I extend my hand for a shake to seal the deal. If the student ignores my hand or refuses to agree, I restate the agreement. Either the student agrees or I say, "Let's step outside the classroom so that we can discuss this privately. I don't want to write a referral for you. I would like you to have the option of choosing your own behavior and consequences."

For years I practiced what we now call zero stimulation, before I knew it had a name. My instinct was to remove the student from my classroom so that he or she would be able to focus on his or her own thoughts, feelings, and behavior. A few years ago, I learned that many psychologists agree that the only effective form of behavior modification is the time-out, which removes all stimulation, followed by a discussion of the specific behavior that needs to change.

If the student refuses to step outside, which rarely happens, then of course I have to call security and ask that a guard escort the student to the office because he is not able to cooperate with me. I don't accuse the student of insubordination or defiance. I simply state that he is unable to cooperate. I want the student to have to explain the situation to the principal because I am aware that the student may be reacting to some personal situation that has upset him or her beyond the ability to cope.

If the student does step outside into the hallway, I wait a minute or two for us both to catch a breath. I make sure the rest of the students are on task. If students appear to be starting to rumble, I ask, "Is there anybody else who needs to step outside for a chat?" Suddenly, everybody is engrossed in the assignment.

Once outside I look the student in the eye and wait for him or her to look at me. Some students are shy. Others have been taught that it is disrespectful to look directly at an adult. If the student doesn't make eye contact, I say, "Please look at me because I want to be sure that we understand each other, and I can't be sure unless I can see your eyes."

Next I say, "Please don't forget that I like you, although I may not always like your behavior. Would you like to tell me what's wrong? Confidentially?"

If the student tells me, then we can discuss possible solutions, and I thank the student for his or her honesty. Then I extend my hand and say, "Thanks for talking to me about this. I am glad that we didn't have to resort to the emergency backup procedure and send you to the office. That would have wasted everybody's time, and it would not help you be a successful student. Next time you have a problem, why not take a deep breath and close your eyes? Or just step outside into the hall and give yourself a minute or two. Just let me know that you're going, and I will talk to you if you need me to."

If the student seems unable or unwilling to talk to me, I say, "OK, you think about your options. I will be back in a few minutes. Please stay here and don't talk to any students who pass by. If you leave, I won't have any choice but to report you for cutting class."

Then I return to my classroom. I may or may not go back into the hallway. If the student seems very angry or sullen or aggressive, I leave him or her in the hallway until the bell rings, although I check periodically to make sure the student is still there. Just before the bell rings, I open the door and say, "Thank you for staying here. That was a responsible decision on your part. I hope that you are able to find a better solution to your problems next time. If you want to talk to me, I will be available."

If the student seems open to a conversation, I make sure that the students in the classroom get my attention first. When they are all working, I step outside and ask the student what he or she thinks about the situation. Instead of accusing, I ask questions: Are you feeling upset or angry today? Are you hungry? Is the work too hard or too easy? Is somebody bothering you? Did I do something to offend you? Are you mad at your parents? I ask questions until either I hit on the right answer or the student tells me. Sometimes it takes a while for them to figure out what is bothering them. Life is very difficult for many young people, and many of them are afraid they will cry if they talk about their troubles. So they shrug and profess that they don't know what's wrong. As long as they learn to control their impulsive behavior, I allow them their privacy.

After years of working with at-risk teens and adults enrolled in developmental-level college courses (the at-risk teens who survived high school), I have come to believe that there is a reason for every behavior. Until we discover the reason, we can't hope to change the behavior permanently. So my first step as a teacher is to seek out the cause. Often this seeking will be so unexpected and engaging that the student will forget to act obnoxious, offensive, and defensive. The moment the defense is down, I nuke them with love and respect. They rarely recover.

6

Dear Miss J

When I was ten years old, I wrote letters to several of my favorite authors. None of them responded. I vowed then that when I became a published author I would answer every single letter from my readers (it never occurred to me that I might not have readers because my fifth-grade teacher, Mrs. Hodak, told me she believed I could write books when I grew up).

Answering readers' letters has never seemed a chore to me—I consider it a privilege. I cherish every one of the letters I have received from people of all ages who have read my books and felt compelled to write to me—to ask a question, to tell me about their most beloved teachers, to comment on their experiences with our school system, sometimes just to share their thoughts with somebody they know will listen and care about them.

In this chapter I have included a number of questions from parents, teachers, and future teachers. Some responses are lengthy, but I believe that people who take the time to formulate a serious question deserve a complete and thoughtful answer.

As I read through my stacks of letters and e-mails to select a good sample, it occurred to me that they mirror the situation in many schools—nearly all of the teachers' letters concern administrative or disciplinary matters. Hundreds of children have also written to me, but their questions invariably concern emotional or personal situations. It seems that teachers might take a clue from the content of children's questions and focus their efforts more on changing the nature of their personal interactions with students. Not that teachers don't care, but given the limited time we have with students, most of us have to forsake the personal and focus on the academic. Certainly, academic instruction is the foundation of any school, as it should be, but before we can effectively instruct, we must address the emotional and personal issues that hold our children hostage. Children's brains don't come to school all by themselves: they bring little bodies, hearts, and souls along with them. And these too need nurturing. As long as we require our children to attend school, I believe it is our responsibility to make the experience enjoyable—or at the very least painless.

My approach is the opposite of the textbook method that many teacher-training programs suggest. New teachers are often advised "Don't smile until Christmas" in the hopes that a firm, unsmiling face will inspire discipline, respect, and obedience. My advice to new teachers is to smile at every opportunity, particularly during the first days of class. Students of any age are far more receptive to teachers who like them. Kindness does not equal weakness. Children know that. We adults need to remember it.

Q: I went through teacher training and I earned straight As. My professors said my lesson plans were great, and I thought I was prepared to teach. But when I got into the classroom, I couldn't cope with all the paperwork in addition to lessons, and I didn't know how to manage the classes. I was so overwhelmed that I ended up taking everything home at night and working until midnight. Even though I taught elementary school, I was afraid to look the students in the eye. I was afraid that they would laugh at me or belittle me. After a short while, I gave up teaching because it became clear to me that it wasn't what I was meant to do. Do you think I was just naive, or do you think my experience was common among people who believe they want to be teachers?

A: I think you have highlighted some of the most important failures in our teacher-training systems. Many colleges and universities have revamped their programs recently to include a heavy focus on classroom management and discipline, so perhaps fewer teachers will face the dilemma you faced. But I don't think your situation is unusual at all. I think the statistics show that most teachers who quit teaching do so during the first five years, for exactly the reasons you mentioned. They can create great lesson plans and learn all the latest theories, but they aren't prepared to face real students who challenge their authority and refuse even to look at those beautiful lesson plans.

Teaching involves far more than being educated and wanting to teach children. It involves a great deal of psychology, leadership, and time management—and the ability to motivate people who aren't inclined to be motivated. Those skills can be learned, but they require practical experience and real-world application. I think student teaching should last at least a full year and should be completed during the second year of teacher training instead of the last, so that teacher candidates can get a better idea of whether they really want to teach.

Q: I have always had a good relationship with parents of my students, until this year. I can't seem to connect with the parents of my kids. Many of them won't even give me a phone number to contact them. And when I send things home, they ignore them. The kids know this upsets me, and now they are upset too. Should I just give up or keep trying to get through to them? A: I spent seven years teaching kids with parents and guardians like the ones you are trying to work with. After hundreds of conferences and conversations, I believe that there are many reasons why parents don't cooperate. Here are some possibilities:

1. Their own school days were miserable for some reason—perhaps they had family problems or teachers who humiliated them or some kind of learning disability—so they avoid being near a school.

2. They can't spell or read well, and they are embarrassed to write or talk to you.

3. They believe they will be blamed for their child's learning problems or behavior. Even though they may be responsible, they don't want to be lectured or shamed.

4. They don't speak English well and are ashamed of their grammar or accents.

5. They are poor, tired, overworked, abused, or something that saps their energy so that they simply can't cope.

6. They really are pathetic parents who don't care.

My most successful approach was to call each parent or guardian individually and introduce myself and provide my phone number and invite the person to my classroom to visit. If the adult didn't have a car, I would try to meet the parent someplace in their community (library, for example), just to talk to them so that they could see that I was trying to help and not blame them.

If I couldn't get a phone number, I made visits to the homes, accompanying the child home after school so that the kid could show me where to go and the neighbors could see that I was a welcome visitor and not some kind of inspector or snoop. If I couldn't make contact with the parent or guardian through a home visit, I asked the child to give me the name of anybody older who might be willing to talk to me—a neighbor, aunt, cousin, grandmother, older sister or brother. Then I would write that person a note and ask them to call me or come visit my classroom.

Some parents never did make contact, and in those cases I tried to find a coach or counselor or somebody to mentor the child. Your attendance monitor or administrative secretary may have a big enough heart to take on a lost little soul. Very often bus drivers develop a good rapport with the kids they chauffeur. One bus driver told me that she always asked to see their report cards and that some kids said she was the only person who ever looked at their grades.

Another thing that worked for me was to hold a parent meeting away from school, at a community center, library, or church basement. Many parents felt more comfortable on their own turf; and when they realized that I was willing to come to them, many of them dropped their negative attitudes.

Good luck to you. Those children are lucky to have you, and many of them will remember you for the rest of their lives—even if they don't realize it now.

Q: I am at my wit's end. I have three children in school, and all they do is test. I have tried to talk to the teachers, but they say there is nothing they can do. They have to spend all their time teaching the kids to take tests. My daughter used to love school, and now she hates going. I am thinking of homeschooling, but I don't know where to get the materials; and I'm not sure I feel confident to teach her. But I would rather try than watch her fail because she hates school. Do you think I should try and, if so, where could I get information or help?

A: I understand your dilemma completely, and you have my empathy. That is exactly why I am not teaching full-time in a public school right now: I just can't bring myself to spend so much time teaching kids to take standardized tests. I think there are better ways to ensure that all children learn. As for homeschooling, I think your success will depend on a lot of things. First, does your daughter want to be homeschooled? It is hard to teach a child who doesn't want to be where she is. Second, do you have other adults who can provide a support network and perhaps some tutoring if you run into subject areas where you might have a problem, such as advanced mathematics, biology, or physics? Third, do you live in a community where social or religious groups offer activities so that your daughter can interact with other children?

I am not an expert on homeschooling, but I believe that most school districts provide some sort of state or district curriculum guide for parents who homeschool; they may not offer this to you unless you ask for it, though. If they don't have one or won't provide one, then contact your state department of education and find out exactly what the requirements are for you to homeschool. Also, you can do an Internet search for sites that provide support for parents who homeschool. Http://www.homeschool.com is a good place to start. If you are not computer literate, ask your local public librarian for help.

Be sure to do a little background checking on any Web site or group before you accept its advice. Many Web sites are legitimate and contain information from knowledgeable and experienced people. But some sites are monitored by groups whose primary purpose in homeschooling is to censor and control every single idea that is introduced to their children. Although you need to monitor information to make sure it is age appropriate and not offensive to you, I believe the parents who try to shut off their children from the world usually do their children a disservice. Children don't simply abandon their parents' values and beliefs because they read or hear something that conflicts with what their parents taught them. In fact, when you run across something controversial, you can use that as a springboard for discussion with your child.

Q: How do you teach your multicultural view to your classes without pushing your opinions on them?
A: I explain to every class that I believe disrespect for others stems from a lack of self-respect, so one of my primary goals is to help them develop healthy self-respect. I tell them that I am passionate about treating each person with dignity and respect. Children have huge feelings, so they understand passion and respect it when it is genuine.

My one classroom rule is this: treat yourself and others with respect. That means no put-downs of others based on skin color, ethnic background, native language, economic status, religion, gender, sexual preference, body shape, or body size. Those characteristics are not ones we choose; we are born with them. I do allow students to criticize each other's logic, politics, attitudes, treatment of others, and so on, because we do choose those things; and it is important to know why we believe what we believe and why we do what we do.

Students understand when I tell them that I want them to see each other and not erase each other's faces by stereotyping them. They also understand when I explain that I believe prejudices are like underpants: most of us have them, but it's tacky to display them in public, especially to strangers. They giggle, but they get the message.

Always I ask if anybody thinks my rule is unreasonable, and nobody ever does. Even students who do have strong prejudices understand that we all want to keep our dignity. If you require students to conduct themselves as though they have self-respect, eventually it becomes reality. Kids have told me many times that they don't appreciate being allowed to act any way they choose, disregarding the effect they have on others. They do appreciate adults who require high standards of personal conduct. They also remind me that it's important for adults to follow their own rules.

Q: In one of your books, you mentioned that you eliminated tests. How did you grade students without testing?
A: I wish I could eliminate tests! At least the standard-format true-or-false, matching, fill-in-the-blank tests and any test that can be graded with a Scantron or similar machine. Those tests focus on lower-level thinking skills and require more regurgitation than cogitation, but they are easy to grade, if you simply want some grades to put in your book. I do believe in tests that make an effort to truly assess student progress, but they take much more time to design, complete, and correct.

I believe a test should check two things: student learning and teacher teaching. If students do not grasp a concept, I am as responsible as they are. Poor test grades indicate to me that I need to make some changes in my lessons and teaching style. If there are many poor test grades, it indicates that my class as a group needs some remedial work to catch them up to grade level. (In that case those few students who do not need remedial work have the option of completing independent writing or library research projects for extra credit.)

I did not entirely abandon tests because I have always taught in public schools, where tests are required. But because so many unsuccessful students dread tests to the point that they sabotage their own scores, often I would label a test as a review or practice test and use the grades as a test grade. I'd give students the option of keeping the practice grade or the "real" grade, whichever was higher. For students who didn't pass the practice or the real test (which didn't happen often), I would make more assignments and then retest them (with a different test). Many students suffer from true test anxiety. When these students know they aren't going to be punished for not being perfect, that their scores aren't permanent, often they relax and do much better.

I believe that most of the problems with testing result from making tests too important; from trick or ambiguous questions; or from tests designed to be difficult but not necessarily a good assessment of student knowledge, skills, or effort. Teachers must take care to design tests that actually provide an accurate assessment—not an easy task.

The testing situation is out of control. Teachers are pressured to spend precious class time teaching children to take a specific test, and schools are threatened with loss of funding if children earn poor test scores. Logically, schools with the lowest test scores would seem to be the ones that need more funding, yet the opposite occurs.

Although test makers have tried to improve the level of critical thinking that tests require, including literary analysis, for example, standardized tests have one fundamental problem: they are designed to be easily and quickly graded, so they primarily test lower-level thinking skills such as recall and basic comprehension. Synthesis and evaluation—the highest levels of thinking—cannot be tested accurately through multiple choice, true-or-false, short essay, or fill-in-the blank answers.

If we truly wanted to test our students' academic skills and knowledge, we would require tests similar to the ones that master's and doctoral degree candidates take. Students would write a substantial body of work based on their research and study; they would present oral arguments and answer questions from a panel of professional teachers; they would complete a comprehensive exam covering several years of study. If we imposed such an exam system, some students would fail. Like their university counterparts, those students would be required to complete further studies before retaking the exam. But we can't do that for our elementary and high school students—not because it would be impossible for them to learn the material and skills but because the goal of our current system is to move students through the schools and get them out, educated or not.

Q: What is the best way you have found to motivate unmotivated students?
A: When I have students who clearly detest school, I make it a point to find out why. I chat with the students before or after class or communicate through private journals until I find out what made them hate school. There is always a reason. Until we know the reason for a child's behavior, we can't change the behavior.

One of my most successful techniques is to offer all students what I call amnesty at the start of each school year. I tell them I don't care what they did last year, last week, or one minute before I met them. I am interested in how they behave in my classroom. If they decide they want to pass my class, I will help them. Every time I make that offer, at least one student stops by after class to ask whether I am "for real." They seem torn between wanting to succeed and not believing such a thing is possible.

Most kids who refuse to try don't believe they can succeed. Or they have a reason for failing, such as trying to punish their parents or hoping that bad behavior will result in a change of custody. Many students honestly believe they are headed for prison, poverty, or early death; so they don't see a reason to try in school. I work to change these students' perceptions of themselves. I tell them that I see their talents and intelligence and that I will help them develop their skills if they will work with me instead of against me. I make the logical case that if they hate school, it makes more sense to pass those classes and get it over with instead of dragging it out for another semester or year.

In my experience poor reading comprehension is the root of most school problems. Some kids who are intelligent can tap-dance their way through the eighth grade, but when they hit high school, they can't comprehend the textbooks—especially math and science—and they can't memorize everything the teachers say in class as they could when the material was easier. Many of these kids will misbehave in order to get out of the classroom, where they feel humiliated and fearful; and many end up in detention centers or in programs for behavior-disordered children.

Early in the year, I explain to my classes my belief that reading skills can make or break a student. I point out that reading is a skill and that nobody ever gets good at a skill they never practice. Basketball players, singers, race car drivers, beauticians—everybody practices to improve his or her chosen skills. I ask them to honestly assess how much effort they have put into becoming good readers. Then I ask them to try for just three months—ninety days. We make a calendar and cross off the days as we read. I promise them that I will work with them to figure out why they have trouble reading and provide help to improve their skills. Most students are willing to try, although some have already learned to hate reading so much that they simply cannot believe they can learn. I continue to encourage those students, but I don't pressure them. Eventually, most of them come around when they see their classmates struggling and improving.

Surprisingly, many students with very poor comprehension skills appear to be good readers. They sound fluent when they read aloud, but as one boy explained to me, "It's like one of those neon signs in front of the bank. I see the words when I read them, but as soon as they are gone, they disappear from my brain."

Unfortunately, many of those poor readers believe that it takes a calendar year to move up a year in reading level. These students need to understand that if they will work with you to determine the reason for their poor reading skills, they can catch up in a matter of weeks or months. I ask my poor readers to give me the benefit of the doubt and to try different strategies before they give up on themselves. I require them to read silently at least ten minutes of every day in every class. I read out loud to them. I discuss scotopic sensitivity (see Chapter Nine) with them and provide colored transparencies to place over their reading materials. I do reading comprehension assignments along with the class and share my thinking and my answers to provide a model and motivation. I let them grade my assignments.

I do not ever, under any circumstances, force a student to read out loud if he or she doesn't want to. I think that is one of the primary reasons why students cut classes and why they hate reading. So many teachers have made reading a humiliating experience. We need to make it an exciting challenge instead. That's our most important job. Good readers are good thinkers, and good thinkers can succeed in any subject.

Q: How do you get students to see themselves beyond being at risk and then to excel?

A: First, I tell my students that I don't like the term *at risk* because it doesn't accurately describe them. All children are at risk in today's society. One boy told me that when he heard himself described as at risk, he felt as though the people were saying he was a hopeless loser. I prefer the term *disenchanted students* because such students have given up on school. Perhaps they are tired of failing or fighting with teachers who don't understand their learning styles. Perhaps they feel like outcasts among their peers, or they are angry about their difficult personal lives. Perhaps they decided at some point that working hard in school didn't pay off. Regardless of the reason why students have given up on school, I firmly believe that kids who claim they don't care do, in fact, care very much. But they have learned to project the opposite image in order to protect themselves from further pain and embarrassment.

The key to helping disenchanted students is to separate the child from the school, to see each child as a human being and not merely as a student. I search until I find some natural strength or skill—and everybody has at least one. I praise the students for their patience, compassion, fashion sense, artistic ability, musical talent—whatever makes them special. I tell them how I see them. By seeing a different image of the child and communicating that image, often I am able to change a child's perception of him- or herself; the child can no longer go on thinking of him- or herself as a failure or a loser or whatever vision the child previously had.

Once I have established some rapport, I find out what interests or hobbies the student has, and I point out that writing a song, lifting a one-hundred-pound barbell, learning to drive, or knowing how to take care of a turtle are all skills that this student has successfully mastered. Then I encourage them to take on academic challenges with the promise that I will be their helper. I start with something small but difficult (learning five college-level vocabulary words or five difficult spelling words) so that accomplishing the goal will result in a true feeling of success. Each success builds more confidence.

One more important thing I discuss with my students is the nonimportance of grades. Grades are important only in a certain context. We all know people who earn As but are not very likable or successful in any other area. In fact, some people who earn As are F people: they have terrible personalities. And we all know people who earn Ds and Fs but who are popular, charming, talented, and successful in other areas; they are A people who earn Fs. In my opinion it is far better to be an A person who can work to improve his or her grades than an F person who earns academic honors. Grades can always be improved; and given the choice, I would opt for a lovely person with lower grades over a superachiever with an obnoxious personality. Many students claim that teachers treat students who earn high grades better than they treat students with average or low grades. If we do, then we have ourselves to blame when students focus on grades so much that they are willing to lie or cheat in order to earn them.

Q: Teaching is so hard. How do you avoid burning out?
A: I don't. I didn't listen when veteran teachers warned me that I needed to hold back, keep some energy reserved, let some things

slide. I kept charging ahead, determined to save every single child I met. Of course, they were right. After five years of teaching non-English-speaking and at-risk teens, I abruptly ran out of gas. I woke up one day and couldn't get out of bed. So I took a break and went back to graduate school for a year. Then I went back to teaching at-risk teens and lasted another year. I took another break for a few years, tried teaching high school again, and lasted one semester.

The last time I taught high school, I realized it wasn't the students who drained my energy; it was the administration. (I know there are good administrators because I have worked for a few, but far too many are part of the bureaucratic bloat that is suffocating our schools.) I simply cannot teach children to take standardized tests. I think the present obsession with testing is wrong and pointless and a huge waste of money, talent, time, and energy. And I believe our children are going to suffer terribly when they are faced with a world in which they must analyze and evaluate and synthesize—and think—instead of coming up with the "right" answer.

When I am crowned queen of education, I will decree that after five years in the classroom, every teacher will be required to take a one-semester break from teaching. They can design curriculum, provide professional development training, mentor new teachers, coordinate student activities and clubs—some work that does not involve daily lesson plans, testing, and grading. Even teachers who don't want a break (I wouldn't have wanted one) will be required to get out of the classroom. Some teachers will decide not to return, which will be for the best. Most will be eager to return, which will be even better.

Q: If you could only do one thing to change our schools, what would it be?
A: I would reduce class sizes. Preschool, kindergarten, and first grade would have a maximum of fifteen students. Grades two through twelve would have a maximum of twenty.

Why? Because children deserve to have at least one or two minutes of personal attention during each hour of instruction. That is not an unreasonable expectation, yet with current class sizes, it is literally impossible.

Children mature at different rates, each according to an individual developmental clock. To expect one teacher to teach thirty little clocks to read at the same time is unreasonable. It may be possible for an extremely effective and energetic teacher, but that doesn't make it reasonable or acceptable.

Teaching well is emotionally exhausting, even with children who are well behaved and motivated. Every additional student in a classroom exacts a tremendous amount of physical, mental, and emotional energy. If we truly value education, then we must value and respect our teachers.

P.S. To any person who believes that teaching is easy, I issue the following challenge: substitute full-time for one month in your local school and take notes about the techniques and methods you used to make teaching such an easy task. Then publish those notes. Millions of educators would love to read them.

7

Truth in Labeling

We are a label-crazy society. Nobody is normal anymore. Kids who argue with their parents and teachers are no longer simply stubborn; today those young arguers suffer from authority defiance disorder. Bookworms and dreamers who prefer the exciting ideas in their own minds are at risk of being slapped with suspicion of autism, Asperger's, or some other syndrome, disorder, tendency, or condition. Kids we once would have referred to as a ball of fire or a live wire are now identified as attention deficit disordered (with or without hyperactivity). Labeling kids has become big business—and a dangerous business, in my opinion.

Yes, some children are truly disturbed, developmentally delayed, emotionally damaged, or simply so different from their peers that they require assistance in order to function in a school setting. But those children are a very small percentage, and that very small percentage should receive the full attention (and all the financial resources) of the special education or exceptional children or whatever politically correct label has now been attached to programs designed to aid children who face true obstacles to learning. But because government funding and other sources of money have been linked to labeling, school staffs are inclined to look for more children to label. The sad reality is that many schools label children because they will receive funding for those children only if they label them; receiving funding for regular functional children is very difficult. So we now have millions of children who are supposedly so special that they fall way below (or way above) the norm.

Most of my students entered my high school classrooms with labels firmly affixed. The classes I have taught were called accelerated, "P" (regular), honors, at risk, remedial, limited-English proficient, non-English proficient, and behavior disordered. Students in those classes were further labeled as developmentally delayed, learning disabled, emotionally dysfunctional, hyperactive, authority defiant, and educable mentally retarded, among other things. Even when the labels were clearly wrong, removing them turned out to be extremely difficult, sometimes impossible, and always painful to the child.

Those students taught me to be very wary about accepting the validity of preexisting labels and to be even more wary about applying new ones. Once affixed, educational labels are as impossible to remove as those frustrating stickers affixed to the fruits and vegetables we buy—the ones we end up cutting away because scrubbing at them damages the produce.

Perhaps the most telling example of ludicrous labeling in my experience involves a fifteen-year-old girl I'll call Suzette, who applied for the at-risk program at a high school where I was a member of the four-teacher team tasked with teaching teens who were not expected to graduate without extreme intervention. Suzette had been a special education student all of her life and had been diagnosed as having a number of learning disabilities. Her attendance was excellent; her attitude was exceptionally positive; and her standardized test scores were not so far below average as to suggest that she could not function in mainstream classes.

"I really really want to be in this program," Suzette said during her interview. "And I know I can pass. I will work so hard."

Because of her excellent verbal skills, her clear desire to succeed, and her surprising confidence (usually students who have been told that they can't succeed give up trying), we accepted Suzette into the program—in spite of reservations from her parents and some of the special ed teachers. Suzette followed through on her promise. She never cut class; she never skipped an assignment; and she never gave up. By the end of her first year in the program, she had earned a solid B average in the four classes associated with the at-risk program: English, history, math, and computer applications. Thrilled with her success, the teachers on our team looked forward to attending the meeting that Suzette's mother requested after we posted third-quarter progress reports.

"Suzette's father and I appreciate your efforts to help her," Suzette's mother said. "But we don't want you to give her grades just because you like her."

Appalled that she would think we had awarded unearned grades, we explained to Suzette's mother that her daughter had earned every point in every class. She worked three times as hard as some of the other students, but she did the work.

"But she can't do the work," Suzette's mother insisted. "She's special ed."

"We know that," I said. "But Suzette is doing the classwork and the homework. And she is passing the same exams as the other students."

"I don't see how that is possible," Suzette's mother insisted. "I think you are setting her up for disappointment by making her believe she can accomplish things she will never be able to accomplish once she leaves this program."

No amount of evidence could change Suzette's mother's mind. Her opinion had been formed and reinforced by years of "expert" diagnoses: Suzette simply wasn't capable of succeeding in regular classes.

Our team members insisted that Suzette could—and had proven she could—keep up with her peers. Instead of accepting our proof in the form of homework assignments, classroom projects, exams, and essays, Suzette's parents maintained their belief that we were giving their daughter grades simply because we liked her and pitied her. When they announced at the end of the year that they were going to take Suzette out of our program, we were dismayed. But nothing we said would change their minds. In fact, because we argued so strenuously, they not only took her out of our program, they withdrew her from our school.

I understood that Suzette's parents were doing what they believed was best for their daughter, but that didn't stop me from spending more than one sleepless night thinking of Suzette. Even after she left, I sometimes found myself thinking of her and wishing that we had been able to convince her parents to give her a chance.

Three years after Suzette left our program, she walked back into my classroom as the final dismissal bell rang. She strolled up to my desk and extended her hand.

"I'm not sure if you remember me," she said. "I'm Suzette, and I was in your program for a year."

"Of course, I remember you," I said. She was taller and even more self-possessed than she had been, but her smile and charm had not changed.

"I just wanted you to know that I have just finished my first year of college," Suzette said. "I'm going to be a teacher for learning-disabled children so nobody can tell them they can't do things they know they can do."

After knowing Suzette and a number of students who had insisted they didn't have attention deficit hyperactivity disorder and had proved it in my classes, I became very wary of labels. When counselors or administrators informed me that a student was slow, unteachable, defiant, hostile, apathetic, antisocial, or any of a dozen other warning labels, I spent a little extra effort getting to know the student and forming my own opinion. Occasionally, I did have a truly difficult student, but those were the exceptions. In most cases students had logical reasons for the unacceptable behavior but had stopped trying to explain because nobody would listen—or because nobody ever asked.

Cody Harden, for example, was a defiant, incorrigible, uncommunicative kid. Or so I had been told by the counselor who knocked on my door to whisper that one of my fellow freshman

English teachers had refused to allow Cody to remain in her classroom, so they were going to suspend him unless I would agree to take him into my already overcrowded class. I asked if I could meet Cody before deciding.

"He's right outside your door," the counselor said. "But he probably won't talk to you."

I thanked her and asked her if she would mind letting me speak to Cody privately. She shook her head and sighed but agreed to wait at the end of the hallway.

Cody was a big kid, nearly six feet tall, a husky blond with bright blue eyes—a little too bright, I later learned, a result of one of the medications he was required to take. I stood and looked at him for a good long while, and he looked me straight in the eye the whole time.

"Are you a jerk?" I asked him.

"What?"

"I asked if you are a jerk," I said.

For just a second, Cody's mask slipped, and he snickered. His eyes twinkled. Then just as quickly, the smile disappeared; and he shrugged to show that he didn't care what I thought of him.

"No, I'm not a jerk," he said, mimicking my voice.

"Good," I said. "Neither am I. So I'm sure we'll get along fine. Welcome to my classroom." I held out my hand. Cody stared at it for a few seconds before he realized I wasn't clowning; I expected him to shake my hand. His grip was fast but firm. I waved to the counselor and ushered Cody into my room.

As the other students stared at the new kid, I could literally see the wall of indifference that Cody threw up to protect himself. He slumped into the only empty seat, which was near my desk, and used his feet to kick the desk back away from the girl seated in front of him.

"We just finished reading *Romeo and Juliet*," I told Cody. "And now we're watching the video. Have you read that play?

Cody sighed and rolled his eyes. "Yes," he mumbled. "About a million times."

"Good, then you'll be able to write a good paper when we're finished," I said. I flicked off the lights and clicked on the video. After a few minutes, I could hear Cody muttering, and the kids around him were clearly distracted.

"Shh," I warned the kids. They quieted down for a few seconds, but then I heard Cody talking again. I tapped him on the shoulder and asked him to step outside the room.

"What's the problem?" I asked.

"I don't have a problem," Cody said.

"Well, I'm sure that I don't have to tell you that it's impolite to talk when other people are trying to hear the video."

"Yeah."

"So would you mind telling me what you were saying?"

"I was just wondering how they could build those big stone walls," Cody said. "I mean, that was three hundred years ago or something, right? And they didn't have bulldozers and heavy equipment, so how did they build those big walls and castles and stuff?" He was serious. He wanted to know.

"Well, I'm sure they used pulleys and fulcrums. We can research that in the library later. But right now I need you to be quiet, all right?"

"Fine." Cody opened the door and went back to his seat. About ten minutes later, he started muttering again. Instead of asking him to step outside, I leaned down so that I could hear him.

"How come all the priests got that same haircut?" Cody said. "Their heads are bald on top and they got that dumb-looking hair around their heads. They all look the same, so it can't be an accident."

"I believe it's called a tonsure, but I'm not Catholic, so I'm not sure," I said. "We'll look that up later."

Cody nodded and was quiet for the rest of the period. After class I asked him to stay and talk to me. His shoulders drooped and he sighed, so I quickly assured him that he wasn't in trouble. I just wanted to talk to him.

"You have an inquiring mind," I said.

"What?" Cody glanced around the room, as though he were trying to locate an escape route.

"You're very bright, aren't you?" I said.

"I'm not stupid," Cody said.

"So why do you get in so much trouble at school? You seem to be a likable person."

Cody shrugged. "I'm bad," he said.

"I don't believe that. I think you might be a little stinker, but then I was a little stinker when I was a kid and look how good I turned out."

"You're weird," Cody said.

"I know, but I'm harmless," I said. "How about you?"

"Oh, I'm dangerous," Cody said. He held one hand up to his head, pistol-style, and clicked the trigger. "Shoot a teacher."

"Why would you say a stupid thing like that? Am I supposed to be scared? Think you're psycho?"

Cody just glared at me.

"That usually works, doesn't it? Scares the teachers so they get rid of you or leave you alone."

Cody shrugged again. "Can I go now?"

The following day I held him after class again, and we had another short one-sided conversation. After a couple of weeks, Cody dropped a bit of his defensiveness and actually talked a little bit about himself. He lived with a guardian who took him in after his mother decided she couldn't handle him any longer. He had been a good little kid, no problems. But then he had attacked his second-grade teacher, and nothing had been right since then. He refused to discuss the attack and avoided me for a few days. Then I mentioned during a class discussion that I had had a teacher who used to pinch our cheeks really hard, too hard, when I was in junior high school and that I had gotten in trouble for pretending to be a dog and nipping the teacher on his ankle. That day Cody stayed after class without an invitation.

"Did you really bite that teacher?" he asked. "Or were you just playing?"

"No, I bit him," I said. "I didn't bite him really hard. Just a little nip, really. But he never pinched me or the other girls after that."

"Didn't you get busted?"

"Yes, I got in trouble. But I had good grades, so they cut me some slack."

"That's what happened to me, you know," Cody said. "When I kicked that teacher. I wasn't trying to hurt her. But she grabbed my ear and twisted it and it hurt real bad, so I kicked her. I was a little kid, and I was short, so I kicked her right in the crotch. I think it really hurt her. But they made it out like it was some kind of sex thing because of where I kicked her. Nobody asked me why I did it. They just kicked me out of school and took me to a psychiatrist and put me on medication and made me have all these meetings with therapists and stuff. And ever since then, teachers hate me. Wherever I go, they warn them ahead of time that I'm violent."

Suddenly, Cody stopped talking. He ran out of the room and skipped my class for the rest of the week. When he returned, he acted out for a while but then went back to slumping in his seat, pretending that he didn't care about anything. He managed to complete enough classwork and assignments to pass the first semester, although he rarely wrote more than a couple of sentences in his journal and skipped the essay assignments altogether.

A few weeks into the second semester, I was summoned to an Individual Education Plan meeting with Cody's guardian, the school psychologist, two other teachers, and the special ed coordinator. After a brief discussion of Cody's progress—he was failing his other classes—the coordinator explained that he wanted me to come up with a plan whereby I could teach Cody to write a sentence and eventually a paragraph. Surprised, I looked around the table to see whether anybody else thought this request seemed strange. Nobody seemed concerned. Cody was staring at the floor.

"Cody could write a paragraph," I said.

"We have no evidence of that," the coordinator said. "And proper paragraph construction is an incomplete objective on his previous IEPs."

"Cody, have you ever written a paragraph?" I asked.

"Yeah," he said. "A long time ago."

"When you come to class tomorrow, would you please write a paragraph for me so that I can show these people that you aren't retarded?"

"I guess," Cody said.

The following day Cody asked what he should write about. I suggested that he write a paragraph about how he would work with a student like himself if he were a teacher. He sat down and wrote a paragraph, then tossed the paper on my desk. It was huge run-on sentence.

"Have you ever heard of capitalization and punctuation?" I asked.

"Yeah."

"Then use them." I tossed the paper back onto Cody's desk.

He quickly divided the sentences, capitalized the first letters, and inserted periods where needed. He handed me the paragraph, which was grammatically perfect and had no spelling errors. I took the paragraph to the special ed coordinator, who read it and then looked at me with tears in his eyes. He hugged me.

"This is a miracle," he said. "Thank you so much."

I wanted to say, "No, this isn't a miracle. It's a crime that the system treats this intelligent, sensitive child as though he were a psychotic homicidal maniac." But I have learned the hard way that such statements make people defensive and end up hurting my students and me—without making a dent in the system. So I teach when I am hired to teach, and I write whenever I can. I rant and rave whenever I have an audience, and I have an audience much more frequently than I would expect. I have learned that I can make much bigger dents from outside the system than I can from inside my classroom.

One of the most damaging labels, in my opinion, is BD. Perhaps you aren't familiar with that acronym. I wasn't when a roly-poly boy in my freshman remedial gangsters class pulled my hair. OK, the class wasn't officially titled remedial gangsters. It was remedial reading, first period of the day, seventeen boys and four girls, all of whom were gangster wanna-bes. They weren't bad kids, but they wished they were. And none of them could read worth a whit. Each day I required fifteen minutes of independent reading at the start of class. Because I wanted these students to see that I walked the walk, I read with them. My seat was in the middle of the classroom, where I read intently, occasionally pausing to laugh softly or turn back to check something I had previously read. I was trying to model the behavior I wanted them to exhibit, and usually it worked.

One morning as I was reading, Lalo Rivera reached up and pulled the hair at the back of my neck where the skin is tender. Surprised and angry, I whirled around in my seat and whispered fiercely, "Don't ever do that again! Don't touch me or anybody else in this room!"

Lalo's mouth formed a surprised circle in the middle of his round face. He blinked rapidly and stared at me. *Good,* I thought. *I scared the dickens out of him.* I returned to my book, and so did everyone else. A few minutes later, Lalo pulled my hair again, harder this time. Angered and surprised by the sharp pain, this time when I whirled in my seat, I shocked us both by clenching my fist and socking Lalo squarely on the shoulder. (No, I do not recommend hitting students, and that was the one and only time I ever did.) Because he was a roly-poly boy, Lalo slid right out of his slippery plastic chair and fell onto the floor. As he sat there clutching his shoulder, I ran out of the room to regain my composure. I couldn't believe I had actually struck a student. Perhaps the stress of teaching at-risk kids had finally got me, as people had warned that it would.

One of the girls tiptoed out of the room. "Are you all right, Miss J?"

"No, I'm not all right," I said. "I just struck a child."

"But he deserved it," Angela said. "He acts like that all the time."

"That's no excuse for hitting him," I said. "And I am always telling you kids that violence is wrong. I'm a hypocrite."

Angela considered my comment, then squatted beside me to peer into my face. "Come on, Miss J. You have to come back."

"No, I don't," I said. "You guys have to come back here, but I don't. I can quit any time I want to and get a different job. And maybe it's time."

Angela chewed on her bottom lip for a few seconds, then turned and walked back into the classroom. A few minutes later, Lalo walked out.

"I'm sorry I pulled your hair," he said. "I shouldn't have done that."

"And I'm sorry I hit you," I said. "I shouldn't have done that."

"Yeah," Lalo nodded.

"Why did you have to pull my hair?" I asked. "Especially when I just told you not to?" Lalo sat down beside me and shook his head.

"I'm BD," he said.

"BD? What's that? Bored to death?"

"No," Lalo said. "I'm behavior disordered."

"What's that?"

"I can't control my behavior."

"Is that right?" I countered. "Well, you've been in this class for several weeks, and you have controlled your behavior during all that time. But today, suddenly, you can't control yourself? I'm not buying it."

"Well, I am BD," Lalo insisted. "I'm in a special class and every-thing."

"And what do you do there? Learn anger management?"

"No, we bake bread," Lalo said.

Later I learned that the BD class did, in fact, bake bread to sell at lunch to raise money for different projects. But I was more inter-ested in behavior than bread.

"You have to learn to control yourself, you know," I told Lalo. "Otherwise, nobody is going to want to be your friend or your neighbor or hire you or marry you. People don't want somebody who can't control himself. I know you're smart enough to pass my class. But I can't have you in my room if you are going to hurt people. So you need to make a decision right now. If you want to stay in my class, then you have to learn to control your behavior. You can stand up, step outside the room, stand in the back, put your head down on your desk, hold your breath, whatever you need to do when you feel like you're getting out of control. OK?"

"Does that mean you're going to be our teacher? You aren't going to quit like Angela said?"

"I'll think about staying, and you think about controlling yourself."

Both of us decided to stay, and Lalo ended up earning an A in my class that year. At first he did have to step outside the room quite often, but after a few months, he just needed to get up and stand in the back of the room for a minute every now and again. After that experience, whenever I had a BD student, I made him (they were always boys, which raises red flags in my mind) the same offer; with two exceptions all of them chose to stay, and they passed my class.

I believe it is criminal to give children an excuse for bad behavior. We must teach them self-discipline and self-control. To do otherwise is to destine them to a difficult life. Perhaps their home life is to blame, as some people believe: their parents don't know how to behave, so they don't teach their children. Maybe so. But I believe that when children reach a certain age, they are able to understand that our environment influences us, but it does not have to dictate our behavior forever. Lalo and all my other BD students are proof that children can learn to cope and adapt—if we teach them how and expect them to succeed.

By the way, for those of you who are still caught up in the fact that I struck a child, I did not take it lightly. I seriously considered quitting my job at that moment, because I do not believe in mistreating children. At the end of the day, I stopped at the principal's office to confess my crime and take my punishment.

"Excuse me, sir," I said. "I'm afraid that I struck a child today."

"Who did you hit?"

"Lalo Rivera."

"Everybody wants to hit him," the principal laughed. "But don't do it again."

I never hit another student, but I did encounter label after label, year after year. Here are just a few.

Jerome, who supposedly suffered from such severe developmental delay that he would never be able to pass the standardized tests, never earn a high school diploma. Jerome, who decided to prove his critics wrong and did. Jerome who cried when he held his high school diploma in his hand.

Matt, who had been placed in a gifted program in elementary school but who insisted that he was just normal. He struggled to pass his advanced placement classes until the tenth grade, when he finally gave up. He began failing every single class, driving his teachers and parents crazy, until they agreed to let him enroll in regular classes, where he thrived.

Marina, who had been placed in an ESL class because the counselors couldn't understand her thick accent. Because I had lived in the Philippines during my years in the navy, I recognized her accent. When I accompanied her to the office and explained that she could speak English, the counselor insisted that she couldn't and had to remain in ESL. I took Marina into the at-risk program, where she consistently earned straight As.

Jose, who had been placed in ESL because his last name was Hispanic. Jose had been in one of my classes the previous year; I knew he was bilingual. So, when I saw him sitting in the ESL classroom, I went in and whispered, "What are you doing in here?" He shrugged and said, "This is where they put me." I asked the teacher for permission to take Jose out into the hallway for a chat. He explained that his parents did not believe in arguing with the experts at school, and it would be disrespectful of him to question

a teacher or other adult. I questioned for him, and he was trans-
ferred to my regular English class.

Patricia, whose name was on the list titled "Students Who
Have Been Involved in a Violent Altercation During the Past
Semester." The list was distributed to teachers so that they could be
aware of the potential problem students in their classes. Patricia
had been stalked by a boy from a satanic cult and had brought a
knife to school in her backpack to protect herself from him. When
he saw the knife, he turned her in to the office; she was suspended
and placed on the list of violent students.

Isabel, who had been attacked by a gang of girls who had
already been held back twice because of truancy and delinquency.
Jealous that Isabel had been awarded a full scholarship to college,
the girls targeted her and repeatedly attacked her, knowing that
even though she was the victim, she would be suspended each time
they attacked her because she had been involved in a violent altercation on school property.

When Isabel came to me for help, I called the police, and she
filed a restraining order against the girls. When the administrators
insisted that Isabel would be suspended again, even if she were
innocent and attacked, we reminded them that her parents could
file a civil liberties lawsuit. (They had no intention of filing a lawsuit, but we wanted to make a point.) Isabel finished her senior year
without being suspended and went on to college.

And Dante, who broke my heart when he wrote, "I just wanted
to thank you because you were the only teacher who wasn't afraid
to make me do my homework. The other teachers are afraid of me.
They think because I'm a big black man, I'm going to hurt them if
they make me mad."

"What do you do when teachers act afraid of you?" I asked
Dante.

"I act like I'm going to hurt them," he said. He laughed, but
there were tears in his eyes because it hurts to be a nice person and
have people mistrust you just because of the way you look. Just as it
hurts when you are accused of lying when you are telling the truth

or accused of doing something you didn't do. The teachers who were afraid of Dante for no reason—and there was no reason because he was one of the sweetest, gentlest boys I have ever met—were guilty of psychological and emotional abuse. They were, in effect, saying, "Because you are black, you are inherently violent, and it is only a matter of time before your true nature reveals itself."

One more story. A counselor at a dyslexic treatment center told me about this teenage boy, who was not my student, and I have never forgotten her story. This boy had convinced his father to accompany him to the treatment center because the counselors at school kept labeling him as retarded based on his scores on standardized exams. The boy insisted that the tests were wrong, but nobody believed him. He was unusual, the counselor said, because most children will become what we tell them they are. This boy refused. He wanted the counselor to test him so that he could show his father, who believed the school's assessment.

The boy took the standardized IQ test under the normal conditions and failed miserably. Still, he insisted that he could pass if he just had more time.

"So I tested him again," the counselor said, "but the second time, I put no time restraints on his test. He could have as much time as he needed. He took more than three times what was considered normal, but the second time he scored as a genius."

How many geniuses are sitting in our classrooms, failing miserably, boxed in by the labels that misguided adults have applied to them?

Let's stop labeling our children and start looking at them as individual human beings, with unique learning styles and personalities. Let's take the millions we now spend on labeling and all the special programs that accompany the labels and put that money into reducing class sizes and providing more personal attention from teachers, aides, and counselors for the growing numbers of students who don't fit our preconceived ideas of how they should behave. Let's treat our children as though they were valuable human beings who are entitled to be treated with dignity and respect.

If we must have labels, why not invent some new ones that more accurately describe today's children. How about Too Smart to be Challenged by Worksheets (TSCW), Filled with Childish Energy (FCE), Coping with Parents' Messy Divorce (CPMD), Flying High on Sugar (FHS), Intimidated by Bullies (IBB), Genius but Needs Time to Think (GBNTT)?

8

Hey Miss J!

Once upon a time, I asked my high school freshmen to begin their daily fifteen minutes of silent reading from books they had chosen themselves. This was nothing new. We started every class with independent reading. But on that day, about half of the students eagerly grabbed their books while the other half moaned and groaned so pitifully that I gave them a journal-writing assignment instead. Among the writing prompts was the choice: What's on your mind? Nearly all of the students who had refused to read opted for that prompt, and they certainly had things on their minds: divorce, poverty, prom dates, pregnancy, disease, cheerleader try-outs, death, violence, fear, basketball practice, anger, bewilderment, breasts, hopelessness, frustration, French kissing, prejudice, sexual harassment, and baby-sitting.

As I collected the private journals, I was so intent on reading snatches of this or that student's writing that I didn't notice for several minutes that nearly all of the journal writers had opened their books and started reading. There is always one holdout in a room, kids who try to turn every assignment into a contest of wills, but everybody else was reading. Really reading, not just staring at the book and counting to one hundred before turning the pages so that I would believe they were reading.

That night I read the journals and was overwhelmed by the emotion those students had expressed in their writing. One boy wanted to know whether I thought he should accept the offer of an older girl who wanted to initiate him into the world of teenage sex.

Another boy spent two pages describing his frustration at repeatedly being pulled over by the police when he was driving his mother's old car to the shopping center where he worked after school. A girl who had recently enrolled in my class wrote about trying to avoid a boy who had been trying to convince her to join his group of Satan worshippers. Every single one of those journals concerned situations and problems that would have taxed anybody's ability to concentrate on something as banal as a vocabulary quiz.

The following day I returned the journals during the start of our independent-reading period. Some of the students immediately began writing more in response to my comments, but others read my comments and then began reading. No moans, no groans, no holdouts. But the next day another handful of dissenters arose to greet the reading bell. Again I gave them the option of writing in their journals. And again all of them chose the same prompt: What's on your mind?

Within a week they had me trained. When they needed to put their worries into writing, they grumbled and squirmed and refused to read. I let them write for a while, and then they read their books. I read the journals and gave my best advice or my most sincere empathy. We became a class of writers and readers. And my discipline problems disappeared. Completely.

When I repeated this experiment with my other classes, the same thing happened. Kids who couldn't concentrate, who refused to even try, would scribble in their journals and then sit down and study. I don't mean to imply that they became overnight scholars, but they did become students. And I became a teacher.

This experience led me to believe that most nonviolent behavior problems that commonly occur in our schools (daydreaming, lack of motivation, apathy, inability to focus) would diminish or disappear if we paid more attention to what students pay more attention to—their feelings. Unhappy and overwhelmed children can't concentrate nearly as well as can children who believe that they are capable of coping with their lives. We can't solve their problems or promise them that everything will be all right. But we most certainly can listen to their concerns, offer our empathy if not our advice, point them in the direction of help, and let them know that other people have faced the same problems and survived.

Nearly every letter of the hundreds I've received from children concerns an emotional situation or conflict with peers, friends, siblings, parents, or teachers. Although some of their concerns may seem small to adults, we must remember that children have big feelings. I remember some of my own big feelings as a child. I worried that my grandmother was going to die from "sugar," that vampires and werewolves were lurking outside my bedroom, that the Communists were going to bomb my school (remember those drills where we had to hide under our desks, as though that would save us?), that we were going to have to move to the poorhouse if we didn't stop wasting so much toilet paper. I'm sure I had a thousand other worries, and I'm equally sure that I spent a great deal of time gazing out the windows or staring at the ceiling, wondering what would become of my family and me. The dangers I envisioned were primarily imaginary, but the dangers children worry about today are very real. That's why I take the time to address their fears—so that they can relax for at least a little while and focus on their school lessons.

I'd like to share with you some of the many letters and e-mails I have received from students around the world. Perhaps their letters will light the bulb about a child in your class or in your family. If you are a teacher, perhaps you could use them as a springboard for writing assignments, discussions, or debates in your own classroom. If nothing else, perhaps you will pause for a moment the next time you begin to lose patience with a child who won't listen to you. Perhaps you will realize that the child needs you to listen to her or him.

Q: There are two boys in our class who beat up everybody and do mean things. They keep picking on everybody, not just me. They are making my life so miserable that I don't even want to go to school.

—Alec, age 10

A: Alec, some silly kids think that if they act like bullies it means they are tough. That is wrong. People who act like bullies are just showing that they are afraid, and they are trying to make other people afraid too.

You can't make anybody else do anything. If your friends or classmates want to behave a certain way, they are going to. What you can do is use your brain. Don't let bullies suck you into fighting with them. They aren't important in your life. Not really.

If kids are just saying things, you don't have to listen. I know it's hard, but if you can ignore them, they will eventually give up. They are looking for attention. If you refuse to give it to them, they will have to look someplace else for it.

But if somebody really picks on you too much or hits you or scares you or steals your things, then you need to tell your parents and your teachers and your counselor. Talk to adults until somebody helps you. There is no reason for you to keep quiet when somebody is acting violent or physically abusive.

Your class has only a few bullies and a lot of other kids. If you other kids decide you aren't going to tolerate the bullies, then you can stop them. Just like in our country. When a few people do bad things, the rest of the people can join together to make them stop.

Telling adults about bullies doesn't mean you are rats or tattletales. A *tattletale* is somebody who tells little things, like when somebody is chewing gum or somebody is talking or looking at somebody else's paper. Those are not important things. So when you tell about them, adults don't really listen. But when kids are being cruel and scaring other kids or being really mean to them, then that is important; and telling does not make you a tattletale. It makes you an intelligent, responsible person. And it makes you somebody I respect.

If your friends want to hang out with people you don't like, then make new friends. There are plenty of nice people in the world. Don't waste your time and energy on people who aren't nice. Think about what is important to you: your family, your real friends, your goals in life, and so on. And focus on how you can reach your goals. That will make you care less about the silly boys in your school. I feel sorry for them. They are weak, and they are trying to make everybody think they are strong. But do you think a truly strong person would act like that? I don't. Good luck and hang in there. Down with bullies! Bullies are cowards!

Q: My best friend Sammie doesn't want to be friends with me anymore. What should I do?

—Danielle, age 11

A: Danielle, I understand your problem. It has happened to me. It hurts when somebody doesn't want to be your friend anymore. But here is something to think about: we can outgrow friendships just like we outgrow our shoes. We like different books and movies and music as we grow up, and sometimes we become different people as we grow. When you outgrow a friendship, it can hurt you and your friend. But sometimes growing up hurts. There's no way to avoid it. It's part of life. When something hurts, we need to think about why it hurts and then just wait until it doesn't hurt so much.

If a friend outgrows you and wants to move on, then you have to accept that. You can't make somebody like you. If you cling to somebody and try to make that person like you, they will probably dislike you because you will make them feel guilty. The best thing you can do is just back off and hope that they will miss you.

Say, "Well, I still like you and if you want to be friends again later, let me know. I won't be mad or try to pay you back." Then go on with your life. Make new friends. Find new interests. Be your own best friend, and then you will always have one friend you can respect—yourself. That may sound silly, but it is true. I had to learn to be my own best friend, and now I really like me. I have fun doing things with me!

Don't talk about your friend behind her back. Just be honest. If somebody says something to you, just say, "I like Sammie, but I don't want to talk about her. It's not polite." Then change the subject. Some people like to gossip, but they don't like people to gossip about them. Strange, isn't it? I don't like to gossip because it doesn't make me feel good about myself.

Here's something interesting to think about: when you are happy, you attract friends. So try to find hobbies and activities that interest you. Enjoy yourself. Then you won't feel lonely, and you will be more likely to attract new friends. It may take some time, but friendship is like a little flower. You plant the seed and then you have to keep watering it and taking care of it before it will grow and blossom. Good luck!

Q: Am I dumb if I can't understand math? My dad says that's the only reason I can't get good grades, 'cause I'm dumb. How do you know if you're dumb?

—Trent, age 9

A: You are *not* dumb, Trent, and it isn't nice of your dad to say you are dumb. Maybe somebody used to say that to him when he was a kid, so he thinks that will motivate you to try harder in school. I think you should tell him that it hurts your feelings when he calls you dumb and that if he wants to help you, he will encourage you to try and love you no matter what grades you get in school. Grades are important for report cards, but it is just as important to be a good person in life. At some time in your life, your brain will switch from concrete thinking to abstract thinking. Concrete thinking is thinking about things you can actually see and touch. Abstract thinking is thinking about ideas such as infinity. This switch doesn't have anything to do with being smart; it has to do with maturity. Just like some boys get whiskers earlier than other boys, some kids' brains switch to abstract thinking earlier. By the time we get to be twenty or thirty, everybody catches up with each other, but while you are in school sometimes things are harder until your brain makes its switch. Think of people as trees. Some grow four feet in a year, and others grow a few inches; but they are all trees when they grow up. They are different varieties.

Q: My mom and dad have been divorced since I was four years old. My mom says that my dad is lazy and irresponsible, but I love my dad and want to see him. I feel put in the middle, because I know my mom is right about him but I still love my dad. I just keep telling myself, "It's not your fault." What should I do?

—Tanika, age 12

A: Tanika, your mom is entitled to have her own feelings toward your dad. Maybe he is lazy, but maybe that is just her opinion. The relationship between a grown-up man and woman is very different from the relationship between a father and a daughter. It is important for you to love your father and talk to him and see him because he is your father, even if he isn't perfect.

Talk to your mother. Tell her that you love her very much and you understand that she doesn't love your father anymore. Tell her that even though he may have faults, you would still like to know your father because you have a little space in your heart for him. Don't try to play your parents against each other, and don't repeat things that they say about each other. Just tell each of them that you love them and accept them for who they are—and you would like them to do that for you too.

Maybe your mother has a broken heart right now, or maybe she's mad and won't be able to talk to you calmly. Maybe she has a hard time talking about your dad, or maybe she thinks he will be a bad influence on you. Why not write her a note and explain how you feel and ask her if she can think of some way you could talk to your father that wouldn't upset her? Be sure to tell her that you love her and you understand how she feels, but that you have your own feelings too, and they are important to you. You shouldn't feel like you're in the middle because the problems they have are between them, and they are not your fault. Good luck, sweetheart.

Q: I read this book in class, *The Skin I'm In*. This girl got picked on because she was real black. She didn't think boys would like her. I feel like her. Will anybody ever love me?

—Cherie, age 8

A: Do you know that everybody wonders the same thing, Cherie? Yes, they do. No matter how pretty or handsome or smart other people think they are, every single person wonders if he or she is good enough. We all want to be loved. Sometimes it is hard in this country because so many movie stars and TV stars and singers are thin and have beautiful hair (or real-looking wigs!). But being thin or pretty doesn't make you a good person, and it doesn't make you more lovable. In fact, look at how many times movie stars get married and divorced. Their lives aren't perfect, even if they have lots of money and are beautiful.

Sometimes black kids get picked on, even by their families, for being "too black." I think that is wrong. I think it comes from the old days when we had slavery in this country and people tried to "pass" as being white so that they could be free.

We are all human beings; we come in many different colors, and all of them are beautiful. Ask the librarian at your school or public library to help you find books that show the wonderful things that black people have accomplished and the contributions they have made to our society. And remember this: nobody can look down at you unless you look up to them. If somebody doesn't respect you, that doesn't mean you have to stop respecting yourself. Just remind yourself that people who try to hurt other people are ignorant and afraid. They have a problem, and it doesn't have to become your problem.

I think the best way to be lovable is to pay attention to your own talents—whatever they are—and you have them, even if you haven't discovered them yet. Maybe you are a good singer or dancer, or maybe you can draw or paint or bake delicious cookies.

Maybe you have a special way with animals, you know how to make other people laugh, or you are a really good and true friend. Find the things that you enjoy and develop your skills and talents, and try to be kind to other people, even if they aren't always nice. When you have hobbies and interests, you become more interesting to other people, and once people know you, they will like you.

Here's one thing you can do right now. (I know this sounds silly, but I know it works because I did it myself when I used to think I was ugly and unlovable, so please try it.) Go and look in the mirror. Smile at yourself and say, "Cherie, you are a beautiful person, and I love you." At first you will giggle and feel silly, but after a while you won't. And you will be your own best friend. That's a good thing to be, because nobody can take that best friend away from you.

Q: I am only one of about twenty white kids in the whole entire school. Sometimes kids pick on me because of the way I talk or the music I listen to. I just want to know how to make them stop.

—Kim, age 11

A: It's always hard to be different, Kim. Usually, kids pick on each other as a way to get attention or to show that they are noticing you. People who truly don't like you usually just ignore you, especially boys. But if they hurt your feelings, try talking to the kids one at a time. It's not good to talk to a whole group because kids act differently when they are in a group. When you are alone with one person, say, "It hurts my feelings when you make fun of me. I wish you wouldn't." Ask them about their favorite music, and ask why they like certain songs or artists. Then explain why you like the songs you like.

They might listen to you, and they might not. They might say they don't care about you or your music. If they keep on teasing you, try your best to ignore them. I know it's hard. Kids picked on me a lot when I was in school. But I finally learned to ignore them and act like I didn't care (even though I cried at home), and they got tired of teasing me and left me alone.

If somebody teases you because of the way you talk or your music, that's not really important. But if they tease you because of your skin color or ethnic background, you need to tell them that they are being prejudiced—and prejudice hurts, no matter what color your skin is. Nobody likes prejudice, whether they are black or white or yellow or brown. We all deserve to be treated with respect because we are all human beings and we all have feelings. Make sure you tell them that.

Q: I want to see my mom, but I can't because they took us away from her because she couldn't take good care of us. Now we live with my dad and grandma, and they don't take any better care of us. How can I go live with my mom?

—Andrew, age 11

A: Andrew, sometimes the courts don't make the best decisions for kids—and sometimes even the best decision doesn't feel best to the kids. Sometimes courts make the best decisions for adults, or they do whatever the lawyer with the most money says, or they try to please the person with the most power. Maybe your mother has some emotional problems, like she feels sad or depressed a lot. Sometimes if that is true, it's hard to take care of children. It doesn't mean she doesn't love you.

I don't know your situation, but I think your first step is to sit down with your dad and grandma and ask them to explain everything to you. Tell them you need to know the truth, even if they think it might hurt your feelings. Tell them that you miss your mother, and ask them to help you figure out a solution.

If you have a special teacher, perhaps you could talk to him or her. You could also talk to a guidance counselor or your school psychologist. Keep an eye out for an adult who seems nice. If that person can't help you, they might be able to suggest somebody who is an expert in handling these situations.

Good luck to you, Andrew. I know this is hard. Sometimes life is very hard, and there is nothing we can do to make it easy. We just have to love each other and do our best. When you are eighteen, you will be able to see your mother as much as you want. In the meantime try to be strong. I know it's hard. But life is hard sometimes, and that will never change.

Q: I am a honor student and I try to be polite and honorable but nobody in my family treats me decent. For my mom and my stepdad, I am nothing.
— Randy, age 14

A: I hear you, Randy. It is so hard to be a good, smart person when you feel like nobody appreciates you. When I was in school, I got straight As and worked hard, but my father always found some reason to punish me. It really hurt my feelings. My brothers and sisters always teased me and called me crazy, even though I got the best grades. They made me feel like I was weird. After I grew up and moved away, I realized that I was really smart and that sometimes people picked on me or tried to find things that were wrong with me because they didn't understand me. Or they wanted to feel superior. That's how people are. You can't make them appreciate you or be nice to you. But you can try to develop your own inner strength so they won't be able to make you feel so bad.

When you are grown and you go off on your own, you will be able to choose friends who appreciate you; I can tell from your letter that you are way above average. It is hard to be smarter than the average bear. Have you heard any of the mean things people used to say about Einstein, the great genius? He flunked math. People called him a weirdo and so on. But he went on and did what he wanted and showed them all.

The kids in school can be so cruel, but that is because they are jealous. They have to try to put you down in order to make themselves feel big. They wouldn't have to do that if they really were big or important. But they know they are small and not too smart, so they try to make you feel bad. It hurts, I know, but if you can manage to ignore them, they will eventually give up and pick on somebody else. One of the reasons they pick on you is because they believe you care about what they think. If you can act like you don't care, it may take a while, but they will get bored and leave you alone.

There are some things you can do to reinforce your self-image and help yourself be strong. Some of them seem silly, but they actually work. I know because I have done them. One is called positive affirmations. You write down on a piece of paper all the good things about yourself. You affirm your value. I used to write, "I am a loving person. I am smart. I am talented in music. I like myself. I deserve to be happy." (Be sure to tear up the paper and throw it away afterward so people don't find it and tease you about that too.)

You can also say positive affirmations in the mirror when you are alone. Smile at yourself. Really learn to be your own best friend. If you learn how to be happy alone, truly peaceful, then you can enjoy other people and also enjoy your solitude.

You can also go to the library or the bookstore and look in the self-help section or psychology section for books about how to deal with people and problems such as the ones you have. One important thing to realize is that you are not alone. Lots of people are treated the way you are, but you will probably never know because they will keep their pain to themselves.

Kids in school used to tease me and call me weirdo because I didn't think or act or dress the way they did. They really hurt my feelings. But I learned to ignore them, and I promised myself that when I grew up, I would show them they were wrong. I was right. Book publishers don't think I am weird—they pay me to write my ideas!

Hang in there and remember: there is life after high school. And also remember that I like you. I really do. When the kids pick on you, think to yourself, "Who cares about those little wienies? I have friends like Miss Johnson. I don't need them."

Q: My best friend always gets mad if I have other friends. I want to keep all my friends. What can I do?

—Rosalie, age 9

A: Rosalie, it might make you feel a little bit better to know that lots of kids have this same problem. For some crazy reason, there are a lot of kids who think that if you like them, it means you can't like somebody else—and vice versa. That makes no sense. Of course, you can like a whole lot of different people for different reasons. But you are more mature than your friends, and they don't understand that concept yet. Try to explain to them that friendship is not like a bag of cookies. You don't use up your friendship by sharing it. You get more friendship back!

When one of your friends complains about your other friend, try saying something like this: "I know you don't like so-and-so, but I do. I think she [or he] is funny [or smart or kind or interesting]. And I like you because you are . . . [fill in the blank with something good]. My being friends with other people doesn't mean I don't like you as much. I like you very much."

If they don't get it, try this: "Do you think that Santa Claus doesn't like you because he gives gifts to all the other children? Nope. He likes everybody. I don't like everybody, but I do like a lot of people. I'm friendly, and I care about people. Please try to understand that."

If one of your friends decides not to be friends with you if you won't be an only best friend, then try to understand your friend's insecurity. Say, "I'm sorry you feel that way. I still like you, and if you want to be friends later, just let me know. In the meantime I wish you good luck." And then go on with your life, and don't talk about your former friends behind their backs. Show them that you really are mature, and try to show them a better way to act. Good luck!

Q: My science teacher hates me. He picks on me all the time. Even my friends notice it. I told my parents, but they don't believe me. They said I must have done something wrong, but I didn't. This is making me crazy.

—Philip, age 15

A: You aren't crazy, Philip. Something is going on. Now you have to figure out what it is. Then you can figure out what would be the best course of action. I can think of a lot of reasons why a teacher might pick on you. Some teachers don't realize that what they consider teasing isn't always taken as teasing by students. So maybe your teacher is just trying to be humorous, get your attention, challenge you to work harder, or show you that he likes you. My brothers used to pick on me to show their affection. It never made sense to me.

If you honestly don't think any of those reasons are the right ones, then let's continue. Maybe you ask questions in class and the teacher thinks you are trying to make him look bad. Maybe you talk to your friends too much. Maybe you daydream or write notes or do your math homework. Be honest about how you behave in science class.

If you are certain that you aren't doing anything to upset or offend this teacher, then we have to consider some sad reasons. Maybe this teacher really doesn't like you. Maybe he is a cruel person. Maybe he's on a power kick. Maybe he shouldn't be a teacher.

I think your first step should be to talk to the teacher. Don't just go up and start talking before or after class. Ask the teacher when it would be convenient for you to have a talk. If he wants to know what you want to talk about, tell him it is personal. If he refuses to talk to you, then you need to go to your counselor and explain the situation. If the counselor won't listen, then go to the assistant principal or the principal or the school nurse or a coach or another teacher. If nobody at school will listen, find a neighbor or a relative, an aunt, uncle, grandparent, or someone else. Find an adult who will listen to you and help you find a solution. Some schools are so small that they only have one science teacher. If that is the case at your school, then you will need some help to solve this problem. If your school has more than one science teacher, you should be able to change classes.

If your teacher agrees to talk to you, try not to criticize him. Try to stick to stating your own feelings. That way you will be less likely to make him angry or defensive. Tell him that you feel as though he doesn't like you. If he says why, tell him. Don't say, "You are mean to me. You are always picking on me." Tell him exactly what he does. For example, say, "You said something that embarrassed me in front of the class, and you laughed. I felt terrible." Or whatever it is that happened. Be specific, but don't accuse him of anything. State your own feelings, beginning with the word "I" and not "You." This is called using emotional intelligence. It's what therapists teach people to do so that they can learn to communicate better. Try to start your comments with "I feel" so you are explaining your feelings and not accusing the other person of something. That way, he won't feel like he has to defend himself.

If you tell this teacher how you feel about things that he says or does, you will give him a chance to explain why he does those things. Perhaps he doesn't realize how his behavior affects you. In that case he may say he is sorry. He may say that he will try not to embarrass you anymore. If that happens, shake hands and thank him for listening to you. Then don't hold a grudge. Forgive him and move on. Be nice to him in class.

If he says you are crazy, that you are imagining things, don't argue with him. Thank him for talking to you and go find an adult, as I mentioned before. You should not have to stay in a class where a teacher humiliates or embarrasses you on purpose. Don't give up. Keep talking until somebody listens to you.

Ask your parents to sit down with you to discuss this situation. Tell them that you are not imagining things. If you have a friend who is willing to talk to your parents, bring your friend to the discussion. Be calm. State the facts. Tell your parents exactly what happens in science class. Don't try to make yourself sound perfect. Just tell the truth. Ask them for their advice and support. Show them this letter, and tell them I suggested that you talk to them.

Another good idea would be to put things in writing. When the teacher picks on you, write down exactly what he said or did in a notebook. Write down what you said or did in response. Put the date by the entry. Then ask a friend who was in the same class to sign his or her name as a witness. Keep this notebook as a record of what happened. Keep it for a while and keep it safe. Don't give it to anybody. If you want to show it to somebody, make a copy of the pages. Keep the originals so they can't get lost by accident or on purpose.

Good luck to you. This is a difficult situation, but unfortunately it happens sometimes. Teachers are human beings, and some of them are more human than others. Try to remember that your teacher is just one human being among the thousands you will meet during your lifetime. You will survive this situation, and it will make you stronger.

P.S. I once had a student who said that the math teacher hated her. I went with her to talk to him. It turned out that he thought she was trying to cheat when she whispered with her friends in class, but she was trying to translate the questions into Spanish so she could understand them. When she explained that she was just learning English, he agreed to help her. Another student had problems with a teacher who refused to read his papers because his handwriting was so terrible. It really was terrible. So I told him to ask the teacher for permission to type all of his papers in her class. She agreed. Sometimes he had to show her that he had done the assignment by hand, and then she allowed him an extra day to type it and turn it in.

P.P.S. When I was in the navy and had a mean supervisor, I would think to myself, "He still has to put on his underwear one leg at a time." It didn't make me like him better, but it always made me smile when I saw him.

Q: Why do we have to learn so much boring stuff in school that we will never ever use in a million years?

—Suzi, age 14

A: I am not going to lie to you and say that you will use everything you learn in school—because you won't. The most important thing you learn in school is how to think, and that's what your assignments are supposed to teach you. No matter what the subject, all your assignments are using different thinking skills, such as understanding, remembering, analyzing, creating, and evaluating. Even though you may not use a specific vocabulary word or math theory, by learning them you are improving your thinking skills.

Thinking is important in every aspect of your life, not just school. Your job and your personal life will require all kinds of thinking. The better you can think, the more successful you will be. Let's say you want to convince somebody to date you or marry you. Or you disagree with your mother-in-law about the best way to raise your kids. Or you want your supervisor to give you a raise. All of these things will require different thinking skills.

There is another reason to learn all that "boring stuff." You have to learn it in order to get your high school diploma. Without a diploma you can still survive, but your life will be much more difficult. Most good jobs require a high school diploma. It takes a lot of hours of study to earn a GED if you drop out of school and then decide later that you need a diploma. I'm sure one of your teachers or counselors—perhaps your parents—have told you how much more money you will earn over your lifetime if you graduate from high school. On the average I believe that a high school graduate earns $100,000–$200,000 more during his or her working career than somebody who dropped out of school. I don't think money is the most important thing in the world, but living a decent life when you don't have enough money to afford the basics is very difficult.

And the final reason why you need to learn all the information required in school is that you are learning to participate in our society. Every goal you have will have some requirements, and many of them won't make sense. But unless you learn to play the game and jump through the hoops and do what is required to get the piece of paper you need, then you won't be able to achieve your goals.

So focus on your goals. Follow your dreams. Realize that there are many things in life that we don't really want to do, but we must do them in order to get what we want. Then it makes sense to do them quickly and well. Get them over with and move on.

The higher you move up your own ladder, the fewer dumb things you will be expected to do. But I can promise you that without a high school diploma, you will end up doing a lot more things that you don't want to do and you will have more people telling you what to do.

9

Scotopic Sensitivity

Alex Garcia should have been my dream student: he was intelligent, witty, well mannered, likable, good-looking, responsible, and considerate of other students. He cooperated with the school staff and treated his parents with respect. His standardized test scores placed him in the top tenth percentile. Alex earned passing grades in every subject. Barely passing. He refused to read one word more than the minimum required to pass any class.

"I hate school," Alex told me when he applied for the Computer Academy, a school within a school for at-risk teens at a high school south of San Francisco.

"But you are clearly intelligent enough to graduate and go to college," I said, thinking that perhaps some strong encouragement would boost his motivation.

"I'd rather go to prison than college," Alex responded. "But my parents want me to graduate, so I need to get into the Academy."

As a student in my English class, Alex participated in discussions, wrote articulate compositions, and listened attentively to other students when we read aloud. During independent-reading assignments, however, Alex became the at-risk, behavior-disordered student that he had been labeled after his freshman year in high school. He drummed on his desktop, hurled paper projectiles around the room, demanded bathroom passes, "accidentally" dropped his textbook onto the floor, picked fights with other students, and defiantly invited me to send him to the office—anything to avoid reading for more than a few minutes.

Because I had the same students for three years and because I spent the first year assessing their abilities and attitudes, helping them play academic catch-up, Alex had managed to squeeze by with minimal reading and a C in my sophomore English class. When Alex started his junior year, I focused on addressing those behaviors that kept him from enjoying the As he was clearly capable of earning.

Alex had joined the Computer Academy because he believed he could succeed in school with the help of our four-teacher team. He had signed a contract promising to stay off drugs, away from gangs, and in the classrooms where he belonged. He maintained that he wanted to improve his study skills and habits. He claimed he was willing to do anything to improve his chances of graduating—anything except read.

"I just hate reading," Alex insisted. "I've always hated it."

"But you enjoy listening to other students read," I said. "You always have comments on the stories. You add intelligent comments to our discussions. You like figuring out the motivation of characters and predicting twists in the plots."

"Yeah," Alex nodded. "But that's different. When I hear the stories, I like them. When I read them, I hate them."

Reading comprehension wasn't the problem, nor was vocabulary, phonics, or any other testable aspect of reading. Alex earned above average grades on every achievement test. I began to wonder whether his previous teachers were right when they said that Alex's problem was power, that he had chosen reading as the one area where he refused to give up control. They believed that because he could read well when he wanted to, he simply didn't want to.

One morning I cajoled Alex's class into independently reading Act II of *Othello*—a difficult task for any group but especially challenging for disenchanted, academically impoverished teens. Two minutes into the silent-reading period, Alex got out of his seat and started wandering up and down the rows of desks, punching other boys on the arms, flirting with the girls.

"Alex, please sit down," I warned in my sternest official running-out-of-patience voice. Alex ignored me.

"Alex! Sit. Down. Now!" I demanded. Still no response.

As Alex approached Emilio, one of my most enthusiastic recreational head-bashers, I could see Emilio clench his fists. My calm, rational demeanor disappeared in a puff of chalk dust. I jumped to my feet and yelled, "Alex, if you don't get your butt back in your seat in thirty seconds, I am going to come over there and kick it!"

Stunned, Alex stopped short. I hadn't intended to threaten him. Threats don't accomplish anything with disenchanted teens, but I was frustrated and tired. I had worked so hard to convince the class to read that I was furious with Alex for ruining the exercise. Everybody else had stopped reading to watch the showdown. When I threatened to kick Alex's butt, one of the girls giggled, which embarrassed Alex beyond his tolerance. He narrowed his eyes and gritted his teeth.

"I could kick your ass," he growled at me. Then he stormed out of the room and slammed the door so hard behind him that the glass in the upper half shattered.

Alex marched himself straight to the principal's office because he knew that's where his defiant journey would end. By the time I arrived in the administration building, Alex was back to being his jovial and charming self. He apologized for his outburst and offered to pay for the window in the door. He shook hands with the principal and me. He promised never ever to challenge me again.

"I don't want to get kicked out of the Academy," he said. "I'll work really hard to make up for this. I'll do extra assignments. Detention. Saturday school. Anything."

"You don't have to do extra assignments or detention," I said. "All you have to do is promise you'll sit down and read the next time I ask you to."

Alex closed his eyes. "All right," he whispered in a desperate little voice.

The following day, when I announced that it was time for independent reading, Alex walked quietly to my desk.

"How long do we have to read for?" he wanted to know.

"Fifteen minutes," I said. I batted my eyes and gave him a goofy smile. "Think you'll die from that?"

Alex didn't smile. But he didn't cause trouble either. He sat down at his desk and read for about ten minutes. Then he got out of his seat, tiptoed to my desk and whispered, "This is why I hate to read." He motioned toward his eyes, which were red-rimmed and bloodshot. Tears streamed down his cheeks. I was astounded. I knew Alex hadn't been anywhere or done anything except read for those ten minutes.

"What happened to you?" I asked.

"I don't know," Alex said. "But this is what happens when I read. My eyes hurt."

"How long has this been going on?"

"Since forever."

That evening I called Alex's parents to make sure they had health insurance. I asked them to schedule an appointment with an ophthalmologist to have Alex's eyes thoroughly examined. I accompanied Alex and his mother to the doctor's appointment because I was so concerned about his problem and I wanted to make sure the doctor took him seriously. After a complete exam, the doctor shook his head.

"Alex has a slight astigmatism," he said, "but there is nothing wrong with his vision. And I can find no medical reason for the bloodshot, watery eyes."

Back at school the following day, I asked my coworkers whether they had ever encountered a situation like Alex's. Some had, but none had an explanation or suggestion. After school I called Diane Herrera Shepard, a friend from Albuquerque who lived in the area at the time and who worked with learning disabled college students. I described Alex's situation to Diane.

"I'll be in your classroom tomorrow," she said.

Diane arrived with a briefcase packed with papers and 8-by-10-inch transparencies in an array of colors—shades of red, rose, peach, gold, gray, purple, green, and blue. She held out a paper on which a series of black Xs formed the shape of a pumpkin and asked Alex if he could count the number of Xs in the middle row of the pumpkin without using his finger as a guide.

"No," said Alex, "because the Xs are moving."

My students and I crowded around Diane. Some students quickly counted the Xs. Several other students agreed with Alex that the Xs were "wiggly." One student said the Xs looked like they were burning off the page. Another student remarked that it was hard to concentrate on the Xs because the page had so many little "white rivers" running through it.

Diane placed a purple filter over the page and asked Alex if he could count the Xs. Without hesitating, Alex correctly counted the Xs.

"Cool!" he exclaimed. "How did you do that?"

Diane explained that black print on a white page creates very high contrast and that people with Scotopic Sensitivity Syndrome find such contrasts distracting, uncomfortable, or even painful. Fluorescent lighting often increases the discomfort because fluorescent lights flicker and don't contain the full spectrum of colors that occur in natural light. By placing a colored overlay on the page or wearing specially created colored lenses, many people who suffer from scotopic sensitivity can read without eyestrain or headaches—even some who have a long history of problems with reading.

Diane distributed transparent overlays, and the students placed them over their textbooks, comparing the different colors. Setting a gray transparency over my own book made it much easier for me to read.

"Scotopic sensitivity is a controversial subject," Diane warned me. "Some people will say it doesn't exist, but others swear that it's real. I offer this to students as a possibility. If it helps them, then I'm happy to provide whatever information is available."

The Irlen System

At that time, in the early 1990s, very little information was available on scotopic sensitivity, aside from the fact that a psychologist named Helen Irlen had discovered a recurring visual perceptual problem during her work with adult students who had trouble reading. The patented Irlen filters and screening process were not readily available to the public. In order to get the filters, students had to have a vision exam to rule out normal vision problems, and then they had to be tested by a certified screener.

Today an Internet search on the term *Scotopic Sensitivity Syndrome* will bring up dozens of sites in a variety of languages, from colleges and universities that have conducted research, from people relating their own stories and successes, and from agencies that conduct testing and training for scotopic sensitivity. The Irlen Web site has an international list of certified screeners and an active patented training program for certified screeners. Rhonda Stone's book *The Light Barrier* joins Helen Irlen's *Reading by the Colors* and a number of publications from Marie Carbo's National Reading Styles Institute. Colleges now offer continuing education units for teachers and psychology professionals who want to learn how to screen students to see if they are good candidates for the colored overlays or tinted eyeglass lenses. And for the skeptics, scientific studies confirm the validity of using colored overlays as a tool for helping readers whose difficulties do not stem from visual acuity.

At the University of Glamorgan in South Wales, scotopic sensitivity is taken seriously enough to warrant this explanation in their link at the university's student services Web site:

Scotopic Sensitivity Syndrome (SSS) has a cluster of symptoms and although little is known about the physiological basis of SSS, it is thought that it is due to the spectral modification of light. That is, individuals with SSS perceive the world around them in a distorted way as a result of sensitivity to certain wavelengths of light. This can lead to reading difficulties because those individuals do not see the printed page the same way as proficient readers do. For example, the page may flash, the words become blurred, move, change shape or reverse or the background may pulsate.

At Piedmont Community Charter School in Gastonia, North Carolina, scotopic sensitivity is a given. Principal Courtney Madden first used colored overlays when he was the principal of a public school. Madden used to gather groups of errant boys in his office every afternoon and have them read to him while using the overlays.

"I was just piddling around, didn't really know what I was doing at the time," says Madden. "I had read about the overlays and got some samples, and they worked with those young fellows. So when we had thirty-six kids last year here at Piedmont who hadn't been able to make any progress in reading, I decided to try scotopic screening as one of many pieces to the puzzle. After using the overlays, all but two of those students passed the EOG [end-of-grade] exam."

In addition to providing overlays for use in school and at home, Piedmont Community Charter School provides a variety of colored papers for teachers to use in making assignments and worksheets for students who use overlays. The children's names are posted above the appropriate colors in the workroom. And because North Carolina has approved overlays for use during end-of-grade testing, students at Piedmont use the overlays during the testing itself.

"I know a lot of people are skeptical about the overlays," says Madden. "They want something real challenging and difficult as a solution to reading problems. And had I not experimented years ago, I would have thought, *This cannot be*. But those overlays have really helped some students who used to earn thirties and forties and are now making nineties and hundreds on their work. In one year our school went from 75 percent of our students passing the state test to 89.4 percent passing."

Charter and independent schools, colleges and universities, and scientific organizations have welcomed the possibility that scotopic sensitivity screening may offer new hope for struggling readers. Sadly, U.S. public schools, with their bureaucratic maze of requirements and roadblocks, and thousands upon thousands of floundering readers, have been slow to open their doors to screeners—perhaps because the schools' fluorescent lights are a primary culprit in the problem area of the reading department. But now that word of mouth and personal anecdotes have the support of scientific studies that confirm the validity of using colored overlays to help poor readers, public schools are becoming more receptive to the idea. Many public schools now encourage their counselors and teachers to attend workshops where they can learn how to screen students, and some schools routinely refer parents to certified screeners as a standard intervention when reading problems arise.

You will find more sources of information in the Resources section at the end of this chapter and in the Appendix, but for a quick look, I would suggest visiting the National Reading Styles Institute Web site (www.nrsi.com) or the Irlen Institute site (www.irlen.com). Both sites have background information, testing kits, and overlays for sale. NRSI offers sample kits of small overlays as well as the standard page-size transparencies. The Irlen site includes an international list of certified screeners and a patented training program for screeners.

Current Research

Dr. Paul Whiting, a professor of education at the University of Sydney, is one of the primary researchers in the field of Scotopic Sensitivity Syndrome. Whiting wrote several papers, including one in which he reports on a number of other published research papers [Whiting, P., Robinson, G. L., & Parrot, C. F. (1994). Irlen coloured filters for reading: A six year follow-up. *Australian Journal of Remedial Education*, 26(3), 13–19].

The paper can be read in its entirety online at *www.dyslexiaservices.com.au/Six-Year_Follow-Up.htm*, but briefly stated, Whiting points out that one obstacle facing researchers is that Irlen filters and formulas are patented and thus not readily available for trial by independent observers (since Whiting's report, the filters have been made available). Studies involved a combination of

Irlen filters, other filters, and commercial colored overlays. The studies using Irlen filters (as opposed to simple transparent overlays) consistently reported positive findings. Studies involving simple transparent overlays produced both positive and negative findings. The majority of people involved in the filter-use studies reported improved visual perception of print, greater ease of reading, and improved written language skills.

Among the studies Whiting summarizes are the following:

In a Louisiana study, over 90 percent of participants who used filters reported improved reading, with 49 percent reporting fewer headaches.

Among Australian study participants 91 percent reported improvement in overall ease of reading; 86 percent reported less eyestrain; 85 percent experienced improved reading fluency.

In a three-year study conducted in four Western states, 86 percent of participants indicated that filters had been helpful.

Whiting's conclusion states that the majority of people who use Irlen filters continue to report improvements. Because my own experience coincides so closely with the published studies, it seems logical to me that all schools would test students for Scotopic Sensitivity Syndrome, just as we routinely check their vision and hearing. But logic so often gets lost in the convoluted bureaucratic shuffle.

Because scotopic sensitivity is still controversial in spite of the growing number of scientific statistics and human supporters, testing students can be a time-consuming and frustrating process. First, parents or guardians must agree to have the child tested and arrange for a vision exam to rule out problems such as nearsightedness. Many schools lack the funds or personnel to attend training at Irlen clinics. Teachers and staff at some schools may be reluctant to spend time or money on a controversial approach to the problem. And sadly, some special education departments resist any intervention that may result in their losing students because they don't want their budgets reduced. They would rather hang on to their precious money than help our precious children—more of a reflection of misplaced governmental priorities than a lack of humanity on their part.

Scotopic Sensitivity in the Classroom

Alex's dramatic improvement convinced me that scotopic sensitivity does exist. As soon as he began reading with an Irlen filter, his reading problems disappeared, and he decided to go on to college (he did earn an AA in Electronics). His grades improved in all of his classes, and he insisted that the purple filter was the key to his success.

Four years later I had moved from California to New Mexico and again was assigned to teach remedial reading. Valerie Martin, a freshman in my reading class, displayed behavior very similar to Alex's. An intelligent, outgoing, articulate student, Valerie complained of headaches during every independent-reading assignment and became a problem student if I demanded that she read silently for more than a few minutes. When I realized that I might be working with another scotopic sensitivity problem, I called the administrative office and was delighted to learn that one of the counselors had been trained at an Irlen center.

The following week, when the counselor conducted an informal test in my classroom, fully one-half of the students in that class responded to the use of transparencies. Seventeen of thirty-four students had been labeled as suffering from learning disabilities or behavior problems—when it appeared that their true problem might very well be perceptual. Although informal, this 50 percent response corresponded with Whiting's estimation.

Valerie responded exactly as Alex had. The moment she received an Irlen filter (hers was such a dark purple that I could not read the print through it), she became the official reader for the class, insisting that she be given more turns to read aloud because she had not taken turns earlier. During class readings she often read aloud for twenty or thirty minutes without complaining of any discomfort. Her grades and behavior improved dramatically.

"I'm so glad I found this out," Valerie told me. "I used to think I was crazy or something because I would say reading made my eyes hurt and teachers would say that wasn't true. They thought I was just trying to get out of work, and they convinced my parents too. So everybody was mad at me all the time, even though I told them that reading gave me a headache. I was starting to think I might be stupid *and* crazy."

I can imagine how frustrating it must be for children to be told that their heads don't ache and their eyes don't hurt, to be accused of being lazy and stubborn. One of the most disheartening aspects of this situation is that when people who suffer from scotopic sensitivity concentrate harder on reading, their symptoms become worse. No wonder so many remedial readers are also behavior problems. Children's choices are limited. They can't demand to be taken seriously. But they can misbehave in school—because standing in the corner or sitting in detention doesn't make their heads hurt or their eyes ache.

After my experience with Valerie and her classmates, I started buying colored transparent overlays at the office supply store and distributing them to all my classes during the first weeks of school as I briefly described scotopic sensitivity. When a student responded positively to the overlays, I referred the student for testing. In schools where testing wasn't available, I contacted parents and provided information for them so that they could contact a testing center.

Because I have repeatedly seen dramatic, instantaneous response to using Irlen filters and other transparent overlays, I am now convinced that scotopic sensitivity does exist and that it may be responsible for many of the so-called learning disabilities in our schools. I believe that if we changed the lighting in our classrooms to natural daylight (by putting windows in our windowless classrooms) or full-spectrum lighting, we would greatly reduce both reading and behavior problems among students. I also believe that screening for Scotopic Sensitivity Syndrome should be a regular part of every school health program.

Resources

For a quick overview of Scotopic Sensitivity Syndrome, the following Web sites provide information, research, and links to additional information:

Bouldoukian, J., Wilkins, A. J., and Evans, B.J.W. "Randomised Controlled Trial of the Effect of Coloured Overlays on the Rate of Reading of People with Specific Learning Difficulties." *Ophthalmic and Physiological Optics,* 2002, *22,* 55–60.
www.essex.ac.uk/psychology/psychology/CLIENTS/aWilkins/Bouldoukian.PDF

This report by a trio of researchers in the United Kingdom concludes with a note that intuitive overlays and rate-of-reading tests are available from the Institute of Optometry marketing department, which raises funds for the registered charity.

University of Glamorgan, Support for Students with Disability and Dyslexia
www.glam.ac.uk/student/SpecificNeeds/spec-home.php

This page provides a detailed description of the syndrome, with testing and support for students.

Irlen Institute http://www.irlen.com.

Maintained by the Irlen Institute, this site provides a good basic overview, including a self-test, questions and answers, suggestions for teachers, and a list of certified screeners and testing centers worldwide. An assessment kit for early childhood screening and overlays can be purchased through the online store.

McCauley Family Learning Center
http://www.lifelonglearninginc.org/mflc.html

Jean McCauley is a former teacher whose center is in Burlington, North Carolina. The site includes a section called scotopic services which has a number of links to further information, as well as information about staff development training for teachers who want to improve their ability to recognize possible scotopic sensitivity among students.

National Reading Styles Institute
http://www.nrsi.com/nrsi.htm

Former teacher Marie Carbo founded this institute, located in Long Island, New York. The site offers a variety of materials for working with readers, information about conferences and training, and products for sale including assessment kits and a number of different sample packages of colored overlays.

Reading & Writing Consultants Inc.
http://www.readingandwriting.ab.ca

This private Canadian consulting firm's site provides good links and information about reading and writing interventions, as well as scotopic sensitivity.

10

The Big Fat Problem

Americans are too fat. We know that. We also know that child-hood obesity and diabetes are running rampant in our schools, along with asthma, allergies, attention deficit, and a host of other learning disorders. Fat and failure in school may be linked, according to recent research. I had read some bits here and there about the effects of nutrition on learning and behavior, and I was intrigued. But after attending the 2003 European Council of International Schools conference in Hamburg, Germany, I am convinced that nutrition and neuroscience are going to change the way Americans view both eating and learning.

News of the Durham Trial

In Hamburg I had the good fortune to hear Dr. Madeleine Portwood, a senior educational psychologist from the United Kingdom, present the preliminary findings from the Durham trial, a research experiment involving elementary school students who were struggling or failing (see page 149 for specific details). Before Dr. Portwood began speaking, I had been feeling a bit sorry for myself for having to spend the Thanksgiving vacation week away from my family. After hearing Dr. Portwood, I was thankful to be thousands of miles from home, sitting on a hard plastic chair in a chilly auditorium. And I was in a hurry to go home—not just to hug my family but to share what I learned with my fellow educators and parents and anybody else who will listen.

First, a disclaimer. I am not a scientist, a chemist, or a trained nutritionist. I have read extensively about diet and nutrition, and I have conducted unofficial nutritional experiments on myself. Some were quite successful. I learned, for example, that if I take evening primrose oil and an herbal complex containing dong quai, chastetree, white willow, black cohosh, and shave grass, I have no symptoms of premenstrual syndrome. I learned that eliminating aspartame (see the Appendix) and high-fructose corn syrup from my diet eliminates depressions and headaches. Since I have no formal background in nutrition or neuroscience, however, I hope that the scientists and chemists among us will forgive me if I simplify for the sake of making a complicated subject more understandable to those of us who don't routinely ponder molecular structure and neurophysiological properties.

Necessary Fats

Fat is a dirty word in most Americans' vocabulary, and that is a big part of our problem. Essential fatty acids (EFAs) are necessary for proper brain function and health. Omega 6 (linoleic acid from plants) and Omega 3 (alpha-linoleic acid from fish and nuts) are both EFAs—*essential* meaning that the body requires them but cannot manufacture them itself. Many nutritional supplements boast that they provide Omega 3 or 6 or 9, but most do not warn consumers that the ratio of Omega 6 to Omega 3 EFAs is the most important bit of the fat picture. The optimum ratio of Omega 6 to Omega 3 is 2:1. Cream, butter, and canola oil all fit that ratio. Those foods encourage proper brain function. Yogurt has a ratio of 6:1, and soft margarine (not polyunsaturated) 4:1. Soybean oil has a 7:1 ratio, and olive oil has 11:1. With these ratios our brains are still in good shape. But when the ratio surpasses 20:1, we have trouble because of the molecular structure and behavior of the EFAs. When Omega 6s are present in much higher ratio than Omega 3s, the Omega 6s will actually block the gaps between the molecules of Omega 3s, canceling the transmission of electrical impulses in the brain, which directly relates to the ability to think, focus, and concentrate. In clumsy, unscientific English: eating too much of the wrong kind of fat makes us stupid.

The American diet includes too much of the wrong kind of fat. Corn oil, perhaps the most widely used vegetable oil in the country, has an Omega 6 to Omega 3 ratio of 56:1. That is more than double the maximum ratio that the brain can handle without dysfunction. It gets worse. Sesame oil has a ratio of 144:1. Margarines and spreads that are 70 percent polyunsaturated have a ratio of 370:1, and sunflower oil has a ratio of 632:1! During her presentation Dr. Portwood said, "Give a child a bag of chips fried in sunflower oil, and a soda for lunch, and that child will be unable to learn in the afternoon."

Dr. Portwood said her research team was especially interested in the American diet because the United States tends to lead the rest of the world in diseases and problems such as attention deficit and other learning issues. She said that studies indicate 50 percent of children in the United Kingdom at age three now show signs of developing behavior and learning problems. Because the surge in attention and focus difficulties has been so sharp in the United States, and now the United Kingdom, researchers do not believe the cause is likely to be organic (within the children). When something happens so quickly, scientists look to the environment for the cause of the problems. Nutrition is one of the key environmental factors. Dr. Portwood says that 20 to 25 percent of neurobiological disorders are metabolically based, which means that they have something to do with the food we eat and the way our bodies respond to that food.

Corn appears to be a major culprit in the United States. Aside from the widespread use of corn oil, high-fructose corn syrup is another staple in our diet. It is hard to find a cookie, cracker, or juice today that doesn't contain high-fructose corn syrup. (In my own experience, high-fructose corn syrup affects my ability to sit down and concentrate; it makes my brain feel fuzzy, and it also tends to cause depressions.) Dr. Portwood didn't spend a great deal of time discussing high-fructose corn syrup because the focus of her research and presentation was EFAs, but she did say that the body can't break down high-fructose corn syrup and that its consumption may lead to weight gain and other health problems. The irony is that many American foods use high-fructose corn syrup instead of sugar and that many Americans have virtually eliminated fats from their diets in the belief that fats and sugars will make us fat. It may very well be the fat and sugar substitutes we eat that are doing the damage!

Mother's Milk vs. Formula

Dr. Portwood began her presentation about the Durham trial by summarizing the results of previous studies conducted to evaluate the effect of different formulas on infants' brain activity and IQ. These babies were not the victims of callous scientists; they were premature infants who had to be fed formula for their survival. The first studies compared two different kinds of formula, one with a superior nutritional content that resulted in significant differences in the infants' mental activity. Then scientists pitted their superior formula against mother's milk, believing that the formula would emerge as the winner. Not only were they wrong, but the babies who were fed breast milk (from their own mothers or from donors) showed significantly higher brain activity and IQs than did formula-fed infants. These results led to more studies to find out what ingredients in mother's milk made such a drastic difference. The answer: mother's milk contains two kinds of Omega 3 fatty acids: arachidonic acid (AA) and docosahexaenoic acid (DHA). DHA is the primary structural fatty acid in the gray matter of the brain and the retina of the eye; and it is important for the transmission of signals in the brain, eyes, and nervous system. Low levels of DHA have been linked to depression, memory loss, and visual problems. The infant formulas contained more linoleic acid and more alpha-linoleic acid than they did DHA and AA.

At specific times (at seven, fourteen, and twenty-eight days), there was a dramatic increase in DHA (Omega 3) in the nursing mothers' milk, which directly coincided with electrical activity in the cortex of the babies' brains. Further research revealed that the amount of DHA in mother's milk varied drastically depending on the mother's diet and whether the baby was born prematurely. Babies born at six months had 50 percent of the DHA of full-term babies. Babies born at eight months had 80 percent of the DHA. This indicates that if the maternal diet is lacking in DHA, then proper levels of DHA will not be present at birth. If the level falls below 50 percent, children have metabolic difficulty breaking down Omega 3 EFAs. And children with Omega 3 deficiencies exhibit symptoms such as dry or itchy skin, eczema, asthma, lactose intolerance, sleep problems, bumpy patches on the backs of their arms, soft or easily broken nails, frequent urination, excessive thirst, dull dry hair, and allergies. But beyond physical symptoms, Omega 3 deficiency has a major effect on children's behavior and learning, according to the research of Dr. Portwood's team and that of other scientists.

Repeatedly, researchers have concluded that Omega 3 EFAs make it easier for signals to jump the gap between brain cells, which helps improve the memory and concentration. Without enough Omega 3s in the diet, the brain suffers, and electrical activity slows down or stops.

Dr. Portwood's team designed the Durham trial to test the effect of EFAs on the behavior of two hundred children, nearly all of whom had problems with physical coordination. Eighty-two of the children had been clinically diagnosed as having attention deficit hyperactivity disorder (ADHD), and forty had reading problems such as dyslexia. Instead of taking a blood test, which would have involved needles and caused fear, the scientists devised a way to use a breath test to monitor the children. Each child was given six capsules per day of a supplement containing a ratio of 20 percent Omega 6 EFAs and 80 percent Omega 3 EFAs. No other change was made to the children's diets. The supplements were administered during the school day by school staff in a blind study, which means that nobody, including the researchers, knew which children were receiving the supplement and which were receiving placebos. Two months into the study, the results began to impress the parents; and eventually they impressed the scientists as well. The researchers found a dramatic drop in excitability and improved concentration among the students taking the EFA supplements.

Further Research

When I returned from the Hamburg conference, I did further research on the Internet and at the library to learn more about EFAs. After reading a number of studies and journal articles, I believe that many of the health problems that plague Americans— ADHD, obesity, depression, Alzheimer's—are directly linked to an overabundance of some fats and a deficiency of others.

Of course, I am not naive enough to believe that one nutritional supplement is the answer to every problem, or even to one problem. But I have read about so many scientific studies in which nutritional changes and supplements resulted in drastic reductions in violent and aggressive behavior, as well as dramatic decreases in ADHD symptoms and allergies, that I am thoroughly convinced: if we spent more time and money on nutrition instead of powerful prescription medicines that can have serious side effects, we would have much healthier children who would be better able to learn and behave in our schools. The only real question that remains is whether we value our children's health and mental well-being more than we value the goodwill of the insurance companies, pharmaceutical manufacturers, and test makers that reap billions of dollars in profits from the desperate parents of children who are unable to sit down, concentrate, and learn.

For a quick overview of EFAs and a list of current articles and research, visit www.fatsforhealth.com on the Internet. After reviewing these resources, I believe even staunch skeptics will admit that there is sufficient evidence to support a nutrition-based approach to the problems of childhood obesity, diabetes, and ADHD.

Resources

"A Randomised Controlled Trial of Early Dietary Supply of Long-Chain Polyunsaturated Fatty Acids and Mental Development in Term Infants." *Developmental Medicine and Child Neurology*, 2002, 42(3), 174–181.

Scientific study of the effects of dietary docosahexaenoic acid (DHA) supply during infancy on cognitive development of infants. Babies who received supplmented formula showed a significant advantage in both cognitive and motor skills.

Willats, P., and others. "Effect of Long Chain Polyunsaturated Fatty Acids in Infant Formula on Problem Solving at 10 Months of Age." *Lancet, 1998, 352, 688–691.*

This study suggests that full-term infants could benefit from EFA supplementation and that effects may be lasting, resulting in higher IQ during childhood.

Beyond Vegetarianism, "Essential Fatty Acids"
http://www.beyondveg.com/billings-t/comp-anat/comp-anat-7h.shtml

This excellent article for the more scientific person provides the chemical composition of all EFAs. Although not simple reading, it is within the scope of a well-educated person who is willing to devote some time to learning more about EFAs.

DC Nutrition.com
http://www.dcnutrition.com/home.cfm

Dr. Thomas Greene, a Texas chiropractor, provides this good primer on vitamins, minerals, and EFAs, as well as links to other nutritional information.

Durham Trial
http://www.durhamtrial.org

Specific details about the study involving elementary school students and EFA supplements, including feedback from parents and children.

Dyslexia Research Trust
http://www.dyslexic.org.uk/nutrition_article.html
Linked to the Durham trial site, this site offers a variety of information and links to other resources.

Food, Nutrition and Agriculture
http://www.fao.org/docrep/003/X8576M/x8576m00.htm
This page from the United Nations multilingual publication *Food, Nutrition and Agriculture* provides a bibliography of scientific studies from around the world concerning the value of fish in maternal, fetal, and neonatal nutrition.

Pam Rotella's Vegetarian Fun Page
http://www.goodfats.pamrotella.com
Cookbook author Pam Rotella knows her stuff about nutrition. She provides an easy-to-understand but comprehensive explanation of the different EFAs and lists EFA contents of different foods, as well as sample healthy recipes.

American Heart Association, "Fish and Omega-3 Fatty Acids"
http://www.americanheart.org/presenter.jhtml?identifier=4632
The American Heart Association provides these recommendations for Omega 3 EFAs, along with background information and links to other resources.

Health from the Sun
http:// www.healthfromthesun.com/EssentialFattyAcids.htm
This commercial Web site provides good information on EFAs, herbs, and vitamins. It also features an Ask the Nutritionist option, access to a health newsletter, and a section on new research with brief summaries of important developments.

ABC News, *How to Get Fat Without Really Trying*
This ABC News special hosted by Peter Jennings explores the question: Should our government protect children from junk food

advertisers? It looks at the ill effects of trans-fats and saturated fats on Americans and explores why our economic system makes it so difficult to improve the quality of our foods. Jennings interviews executives from a variety of food manufacturers and advertisers and shows us just how far those companies will go to make a dollar, although they are fully aware that their products are major contributors to epidemic rates of obesity and diabetes. The special aired on December 7, 2003; videotape or DVD copies are available from www.ABCNewsstore.com (click on "Home Videos").

11

Why I Wouldn't Give My Own Kid Ritalin

A student in my junior English class, Joseph was tall, thin, quiet, and very well mannered, with a string of *goods* following his name: good attendance, motivation, attitude, cooperation, and peer acceptance. But his spelling was atrocious, and from his first writing sample I realized that Joseph was severely dyslexic. He did write in his journal along with the class, and he struggled to complete a few paragraphs while the other students wrote the two-page essays I required of all my juniors. Joseph's writing was difficult to read, but the ideas expressed in his illegible essays were good ones. After working with him for a brief time, I waived the requirement for spelling tests and began quizzing him orally instead of asking him to complete written exams. Joseph was clearly learning the required material and mastering all of the skills that didn't involve writing.

During the second quarter of that year, I assigned a major project for all my juniors. They were to read a novel (half of the reading to be done in class so that I could monitor their progress and make sure they were reading and not simply searching for literary analysis on the Internet). After completing the reading, they had to develop and write a thesis on the book and then create some sort of visual to present to the rest of the class along with a brief description of their novel. Joseph worked harder than any of the other students on the assignment. Often he spent the entire fifty-minute class period reading. But unlike many of the other students, Joseph didn't choose a short novel or an easy one. He read *The Hobbit*. And because he finished ahead of so many of the other students, he read *The Lord of the Rings* as well. I knew he was reading the book because he often stopped before or after class to discuss the books with me (this was in the early 1990s, long before the movie adaptations were made). When I realized we had a mutual love for J.R.R. Tolkien's writing, I had brought in my own set of the trilogy for Joseph to borrow.

When we finished the novel project, the students moved on to short stories. In small groups they were to read four short stories, compare and evaluate them, design some sort of system or rubric to demonstrate their evaluation criteria, and create a visual for a group presentation to the class. Joseph participated in his group's discussions, and he submitted his own painstakingly written literary criticisms. When called upon to present their evaluation, the other students in his group shrank into their seats, so Joseph presented and explained the poster showing how they had evaluated the stories. He was so proud of his efforts and even prouder of the B he earned on his first-semester report card.

One afternoon, a week after report cards were issued, Joseph's mother appeared in my doorway after school. I could hear Joseph outside whispering, "Mom, you're embarrassing me." She tried to pull him into the room, but he refused to come.

When I invited Joseph's mother to sit down, she sat in one of the student desks but didn't smile at me as I had expected. Instead, she frowned and demanded to know why her son had received a B in my class. I assumed she was disappointed, as many parents are, that her child hadn't earned an A.

"B is a very good grade," I said. "I wish I had more students like Joseph. He never misses class. He does every assignment. He works very hard. He's intelligent. And he's very likable. He has excellent manners, and you deserve the credit for that." She nodded to acknowledge the compliment but still frowned.

"But how can he earn a B when he can't spell?" she asked.

"I don't give him spelling tests," I said.

"But you teach English. Don't you have to give him spelling tests?"

"I don't know whether I have to or not," I admitted. "I just don't. He can't spell. Making him take a spelling test would be like making a kid with one leg run a race. He can't win. So why make him do it in the first place?"

"Well, I suppose," she said. "But I don't see how he could pass the other assignments."

I described his efforts on the novel project and showed her his journals and essays. I explained that he took his exams orally because he had difficulty writing the required essays and thesis papers. I told her how he had single-handedly made his short story team look good.

"I don't know how he could read a novel," she said. "You know he's ADHD."

At that time I knew that ADD meant attention deficit disorder, but I was not familiar with the term *ADHD*, so I asked her to explain.

"He's hyperactive," she said. "He's so jumpy, he can't sit still and focus on anything for more than a couple of minutes. He just can't concentrate."

"Well, that's not true in my class," I said. "I have watched him sit here and read for forty-five minutes at a time. And sometimes I had to remind him to stop reading because the bell was going to ring."

She sat back and crossed her arms and looked at me, clearly trying to decide whether to believe me. Finally, she smiled.

"Well, he's been refusing to take that medicine. But I just thought he was being a teenager."

After Joseph's mother left, I went to the public library and searched for more information on ADD and learned that it could be present without or without hyperactivity, hence the ADHD. Some kids can't pay attention, and some kids can't sit still. *Big news,* I thought, *nothing has changed since I was in school a hundred years ago.*

What I Read

I soon learned that things had changed very much indeed since my own school days when aspirin was the strongest stuff the school nurse had in her medicine cabinet. Joseph was the first of many kids who came into my classroom with the ADD-ADHD question hovering over their heads. And like Joseph, many of those children insisted that there was nothing wrong with them, they didn't need to be medicated—and in my classroom they proved that they could sit down and study, although the effort exhausted some of them. Because so many children defied their labels, I continued my research.

The more I read, the more concerned I became that there was so much ambiguity and so much conflicting information. The diagnosis of ADD-ADHD is very subjective and based on a list of symptoms that all children exhibit at one time or another. At some point those normal behaviors apparently became abnormal, but nobody could agree at what point. One expert claimed ADD was a mental illness, but another asserted that it was the result of a combination of environmental factors. Each resource led to other resources. After a few years, I had gathered a fat file folder stuffed with journal articles; abstracts of research results; and links to Web sites, support groups, medical doctors, mental health practitioners, scientists, authors, and grassroots organizations—all with their own arguments for or against medicating children who struggled to pay attention in school.

During the early 1990s, most of the information published about ADD-ADHD concerned diagnosis and medication. In the mid-1990s alarms began sounding from a disparate array of sources expressing concern (or outrage) over the large numbers of children being diagnosed and questioning the safety of pharmaceuticals such as methylphenidate (Ritalin and Concerta) and amphetamine (Dexedrine and Adderall). The United Nations issued a warning in 1996 concerning the dramatic increase in the use and marketing of methylphenidate. I read documented reports of children having seizures, heart attacks, suicidal or homicidal episodes, depressions, stomach aches, headaches, stunted growth, sleep problems, uncontrollable tics, rashes, and a host of other ailments that researchers attributed to ADD-ADHD medications.

In December 2000 (Issue #30) Impact Press published an article by Gemma Hughes entitled "Have You Had Your Ritalin Today?" that hit hard at the heart of the controversy.[1] Hughes explained how Ritalin works; quoted convincingly from the Merrow Report's investigative piece *A.D.D. A Dubious Diagnosis*, which aired on PBS; and suggested that many kids who are diagnosed as ADHD are actually gifted—an idea that I heard again and again from teachers and counselors. Hughes cut straight to the heart of the problem when she expressed her concern that the very people who treat disorders are the same ones who officially define those disorders. Ask an orthodontist if a child needs braces.

In 2002 I came across the abstract from a research study that a group of scientists at Brookhaven National Laboratory in New York conducted, titled "Methylphenidate and Cocaine Have a Similar In vivo Potency to Block Dopamine Transporters in the Human Brain."[2] I was incredulous.

Could this possibly be true? I wondered. *Would we spend incredible amounts of time, energy, and money trying to stop people from using cocaine, only to turn around and prescribe drugs to our schoolchildren that have a similar effect on the central nervous system and brain?* As a former military journalist, I knew that in order to find facts, I needed to go to the original source and not rely on other people's presentations of "truth." So I went to the U.S. Drug Enforcement Administration (DEA) Web site and searched on the word *methylphenidate*.[3] What I read on the DEA Web site increased my concern. Here's what I read: "Methylphenidate, a Schedule II substance, has a high potential for abuse and produces the same effects as cocaine or the amphetamines."

---

1.   Gemma Hughes, "Have You Had Your Ritalin Today?" http://www.impactpress.com/articles/decjan01/ritalin120101.html, December 2000.

2.   Abstract can be accessed at www.biopsychiatry.com/methcoke.htm or via the National Library of Medicine site www.ncbi.nlm.nih.gov. Publication info: Volkow, ND and others, Life Sciences 1999:65(1); PL7-12].

3.   U.S. Drug Enforcement Administration (DEA), http://www.dea.gov.

I subsequently learned from the DEA site that Schedule II substances are those that have a high potential for addiction or abuse, that the U.S. manufactures and consumes 85 percent of the world's supply of methylphenidate—five times more than the rest of the world combined—and that methylphenidate production increased by 600 percent between 1990 and 2002. Those statistics were part of the May 16, 2000, congressional testimony of Terrance Woodworth, DEA deputy director, Office of Diversion Control, before the Committee on Education and the Workforce: Subcommittee on Early Childhood, Youth and Families (www.usdoj/gov/dea/pubs/cngrtest/ct051600.htm). Further along in my reading of Woodworth's testimony, I came upon the following statements:[4] "Extensive scientific literature spanning over 30 years of research unequivocally indicates that both methylphenidate and amphetamine have high abuse liabilities. . . . they will substitute for each other and for cocaine in a number of paradigms in both animal and human subjects; in clinical studies they produce behavioral, psychological, subjective and reinforcing effects similar to cocaine; chronic high dose administration of either drug in animals produces psychomotor stimulant toxicity including weight loss, stereotypic movements and death."

The evidence began to fall heavily into the con side of the ADHD controversy, supporting the claims of the alarmists. After explaining that American doctors widely use only two controlled substances to treat young children (methylphenidate, commonly known as Ritalin or Concerta, and amphetamine, marketed as Adderall and Dexedrine), Woodworth stated, "In 1995, in response to a petition by Children and Adults with Attention Deficit Disorder (CHADD) and the American Academy of Neurology to lower the regulatory controls on methylphenidate, the DEA con-

---

4.   Terrance Woodworth, DEA deputy director, Office of Diversion Control, May 16, 2000, congressional testimony before the Committee on Education and the Workforce: Subcommittee on Early Childhood, Youth and Families. www.usdoj/gov/dea/pubs/cngrtest/ct051600.htm.

ducted an extensive review of the use, abuse liability, actual abuse, diversion and trafficking of methylphenidate. The CHADD petition characterized methylphenidate as a mild stimulant with little abuse potential—this is not what our review found and the petitioners subsequently withdrew their petition."

Woodworth said that a summary of the DEA data gathered about Ritalin and similar drugs showed the following:

> Studies to determine the long-term effects of these drugs are very limited.
>
> No other country in the world uses these drugs to address childhood behaviors the way we do here in the United States.
>
> A number of "questionable practices" have led to the widespread abuse of stimulants prescribed for ADHD, including improper diagnosis, lax handling of the drugs, and lack of adequate information to youth, parents, and schools.

Further in his testimony, Woodworth presented statistics and figures about production, distribution, and prescription of methylphenidate and amphetamine. Between 1991 and 1999, domestic sales of methylphenidate increased by 500 percent; at the same time, the sales of amphetamine increased by more than 2000 percent. And 80 percent of the prescriptions for both substances are written for children with ADHD, half of those prescriptions written by pediatricians. The number of methylphenidate prescriptions rose sharply in the early 1990s and leveled off at about eleven million per year for the four years preceding Woodworth's testimony in May 2000. Amphetamine prescriptions (primarily Adderall) increased dramatically since 1996 to approximately six million.

Perhaps the most alarming of many alarming statements in Woodworth's testimony were these two: "In 1998, IMS [a national prescription auditing firm] estimated that about 40 percent of all prescriptions for ADHD were written for children three to nine years of age and 4,000 methylphenidate prescriptions were written for children two years of age or less. It should be noted that methylphenidate is not approved for use in children under six years of age because safety and efficacy have not been established."

Now, after more than a decade of research, I have become a little cynical and more than a little frightened about the future of the children who are currently being medicated. So many people with so much to gain seem to be willing to use an entire generation of innocent children as guinea pigs. In February 2004, when I read that the government intended to approve the use of growth hormones for children, my first thought was this: *Is this approval for the benefit of children or for the benefit of pharmaceutical companies whose products stunt children's growth?*

Recently, I heard a television ad that touted Strattera (a brand name for atomoxetine) as the first nonstimulant medication for ADHD. I was excited. I thought that the medical and pharmaceutical industries had finally listened to the millions of parents and children who were frightened by the side effects of methylphenidate and amphetamine. But when I did an Internet search, the first Web site I visited (http://strattera.addhelpsite.com) listed the following possible side effects for atomoxetine: upset stomach, vomiting, weight loss, constipation, mood swings, irritability, dizziness, and sleep problems. The second site, hosted by Dr. Lawrence Diller, included an article entitled "Strattera: Now Playing Everywhere," (www.docdiller.com/article.php?op=Print&sid=89) in which he criticizes the pharmaceutical industry for launching this so-called new drug, which the manufacturer has marketed and promoted to doctors for two years in the hopes that the publicity would create a box office hit.[5] Dr. Diller does not believe Strattera has a bright future as an effective treatment for ADHD, in spite of the hype.

---

5.   Lawrence Diller, "Strattera: Now Playing Everywhere." www.docdiller.com/article.php?op=Print&sid=89.

What I Still Don't Understand

My initial question has been answered: yes, Americans are giving their children drugs as potentially deadly as cocaine. And now I wonder: *Why?* Various authors, philosophers, teachers, parents, and concerned citizens offer the following possible reasons.

Money. I did the math. Eighty percent of seventeen million is 13.6 million. At an average cost of $30 per month per prescription, Americans (or their insurance companies) are doling out over $400 million per year on drugs for children diagnosed as ADD-ADHD. As a teacher, I can't help but wonder how many of those children would have thrived if those hundreds of millions had been spent on classroom materials and aides for teaching them instead of on drugs for medicating them.

More Money. Many school districts receive funding for children who are diagnosed with any learning disability or deficiency. And various experts make good money from testing, diagnosing, and treating children who are labeled ADD-ADHD.

Guilt. Parents and teachers don't have to feel guilty about not being able to handle difficult children if those children are diagnosed as ADD-ADHD. Parents don't have to feel guilty about not providing a balanced, nutritious diet or ensuring that their children get enough sleep. Teachers don't have to wonder whether they are boring or deficient in leadership and management skills.

Publicity. CHADD, the largest ADD support group, produced a promedication videotape that teachers widely distributed and viewed—*before* it became public knowledge that CHADD had received over $800,000 in funding from the pharmaceuticals giant that manufactures Ritalin, Ciba-Geigy (now Novartis). When this potentially biased business deal came to light, many organizations withdrew their endorsements of the video, but nobody sent out a new video suggesting alternative treatments. The pharmaceutical ball was already rolling fast.

Ignorance. Many parents are uneducated or miseducated about the drugs that various experts recommend for their children. And many parents trust doctors and school personnel more than their own good instincts. Sometimes parents feel strong pressure to accept a given diagnosis or label. Parents need to maintain high expectations for their children and research any special program or medication that is suggested by teachers, counselors, or medical professionals before they commit their children to a course of treatment or teaching. There is nothing wrong with asking questions and expecting clear, honest answers. Reputable, ethical professionals should welcome parents' questions and concerns as indications that they are involved in their children's schooling and concerned about their mental and physical health.

Convenience. If the kids are on medication, teachers don't have to spend so much time on classroom management. Administrators don't have to deal with teachers sending so many unruly students to the office. Parents don't have to spend as much time meeting and working with school personnel.

Power. Many people believe that society must curtail children's energy, creativity, and imagination for society's good; they believe the maverick must be tamed. (Fortunately, Einstein's teachers didn't have the option of recommending drugs to make him sit down and act like a "normal" child.) Some school districts resent parental interference and find that requiring those parents to medicate their troublesome children gives schools the upper hand. Some schools have even taken parents to court in order to force them to medicate their children or risk losing them.

Today newer and more difficult questions keep me up nights:

Is ADD the result of a brain disorder? Or is it caused by environmental factors such as improper nutrition, sleep deprivation, food allergies, sensitivities to food dyes and chemical preservatives, outdated teaching methods, and overcrowded classrooms?

How can we help children who can't seem to sit still, listen effectively, or control their own behavior without doing them harm?

Is medicating so many children really the best we can do?

Why I Still Have Hope

When I began my research in 1990, I admit I was searching for information to back my own bias against medicating children. As a proponent of natural holistic health practices, I didn't believe any child should be medicated, especially against his or her will. But after a decade of reading, listening, watching, and thinking, I have joined the ranks of the perpetual questioners who believe that a very small number of children can benefit from medications. Those children should be monitored closely to make sure that the drugs they are required to take are helping and not hurting them. But I agree with the throngs of doctors, mental health practitioners, scientists, teachers, and parents that medicating children should be our very last resort—instead of our very first. To believe otherwise is to ignore all the evidence that environmental factors are responsible for many of the problems that plague our children. Researchers have proven that food dyes, chemical preservatives, toxic metals, pesticide residues, and deficiencies of vitamins and minerals all have serious negative effects on brain function and behavior. Nutritionists have proved that changing children's diets can cause significant differences in how well—or poorly—children think and behave. Therapists have produced truly amazing and heartening results using biofeedback and neurofeedback. EGG Spectrum International, an educational and research institution, maintains a Web site (http://www.eegspectrum.com) that high-lights impressive and encouraging case histories, although they are actual clinical cases and not large-scale controlled studies. Some states have introduced or passed legislation that prohibits schools from forcing parents to medicate their children. Some, such as Colorado, have passed resolutions that discourage teachers from recommending medical evaluations for ADHD. Citizen groups such as Texans for Safe Education are taking a stand.[6]

I believe that enough people are now aware of the dangers of medicating so many children and interested in finding alternative solutions that we are going to see more safe and effective approaches to helping students focus on learning. My own answer to the ADHD dilemma is multifold. Parents need nutrition education and assistance in developing healthier diets and sleeping habits for their children; school districts must reduce class sizes so that teachers have the time and energy required to give individual attention to students who are struggling; schools of education must train teachers to be more flexible in their attitudes and teaching styles—and they must have aides and resources available to help with truly unruly children; schools must stop selling out to soda and candy corporations that want to make money at the cost of children's health; researchers must conduct numerous objective long-term studies before the U.S. Food and Drug Administration approves and doctors prescribe any medication for children; companies that manufacture drugs must be prohibited from and severely punished for influencing the testing and diagnosis of any condition that might result in medicating children; we must treat children with the dignity and respect owed to every human being. Most important, we must remember that children learn by exploring the world, not by sitting still with their imaginations disengaged and their hands neatly folded in their laps.

---

6.   Texans for Safe Education, www.wildestcolts.com/safeEducation/safe.html.

Top Fifteen Picks

Here are my top fifteen picks—the most thought-provoking, informative, and intriguing Web sites, studies, and books I encountered in my search for information about ADD-ADHD.

Born to Explore! The Other Side of ADD
http://www.borntoexplore.org

Teresa Gallagher, an environmental scientist who homeschools her two children, posts information on this site "about creativity, learning styles and giftedness to counter the idea that all those kids labeled with attention deficit disorder actually have something wrong with them." This site has nutritional and scientific information presented in everyday language. It links to an array of resources, book reviews, inspirational quotations, articles, and essays—including one entitled "The Problem with CHADD" that provides one of the more balanced critiques of the organization.

Null, G. "The Drugging of Our Children"
http://www.garynull.com/Documents/ADHD/DruggingOur
Children2.htm

Null is the host of *Natural Living*, the longest-running health talk show on radio, a best-selling author of over seventy books, and a documentary filmmaker. His Web site includes a huge library of articles, many taken from medical journals.

Click on the tabs for library, issues, and resources for very useful information. ADHD is the first on a list of issues that includes fluoridation, genetic engineering, pesticide spraying, and vaccinations. The site also includes links to government representatives and other organizations interested in hearing from consumers.

Freed, J., and Parsons, L. *Right-Brained Children in a Left-Brained World: Unlocking the Potential of Your ADD Child* (Fireside, 1998).

If parents have time to read only one book about ADD-ADHD, I would recommend this one. Freed is a former teacher who now works exclusively with ADD and gifted children as an educational therapist. His perspective is logical and humane; parents who want to help their children can easily adapt it. Freed is not completely against drugs. He believes that a small number of children can benefit from medication, but his focus is on finding other solutions if possible. He discusses different medications and diets, but as the subtitle of his book implies, he is more concerned with helping parents unlock the potential of their ADD children.

Eberstadt, M. "Why Ritalin Rules." *Policy Review,* 1999, 94. http://www.policyreview.org/apr99/eberstadt_print.html

This informative and entertaining article details the rise of Ritalin and the backlash against it. This is a very readable account with a lot of interesting side notes and addenda, such as the test scores of a variety of people who took an ADD questionnaire. The questionnaire is reproduced in the article so you can see how you would score.

www.ncbi.nlm.nih.gov/entrez/query.fcgi?cmd=Retrieve&db=Pub Med&list_uids=12737097&dopt=Abstract

The abstract for "Nutrition in the Treatment of Attention-Deficit Hyperactivity Disorder: A Neglected But Important Aspect" reads: "Attention-deficit hyperactivity disorder (ADHD) is multidetermined and complex, requiring a multifaceted treatment approach. Nutritional management is one aspect that has been relatively neglected to date. Nutritional factors such as food additives, refined sugars, food sensitivities/allergies, and fatty acid deficiencies have all been linked to ADHD. There is increasing evidence that many children with behavioral problems are sensitive to one or more food components that can negatively impact their behavior. Individual response is an important factor for determining the proper approach in treating children with ADHD. In general, diet modification plays a major role in the management of ADHD and should be considered as part of the treatment protocol."

PBS Frontline, *Medicating Kids: A Report on Parents, Educators and Doctors Trying to Make Sense of a Mysterious and Controversial Medical Diagnosis: ADHD*
http://www.pbs.org/wgbh/pages/frontline/shows/medicating/

This PBS Frontline documentary interviewed children on medication, their parents, teachers, and experts with vastly diverging opinions. This was the program that publicized the connection between CHADD and the pharmaceutical corporation that funded the group's pro-Ritalin videotape. A printable transcript of the program is available to consumers free of charge, and the archive lists a number of documentaries about ADD-ADHD.

ADD Action Group
http://www.addgroup.org

This nonprofit helps people find alternative solutions for dealing with ADD, learning differences, dyslexia, and autism. This Web site offers some things that others don't, such as a twenty-six-page catalog of video- and audiotapes. Note the helpful FAQ section and the useful list of recommended articles and books.

Feingold Association of the United States
http://www.feingold.org/home.html

The Feingold diet was originally designed for people with allergies until people noticed that putting children on the diet reduced or eliminated ADHD behavior. One of the major culprits, according to the Feingold Association is salicylates, a group of chemicals related to aspirin. You don't have to give up sugar or snack foods on this diet, but you do have to read the labels before you buy. The site provides a list of acceptable foods you can find in your local grocery store, from ice cream and cereal to frozen waffles and chips. Success stories are heartening, and many parents swear by the diet. (Many people find it difficult to follow the diet consistently, but I believe that eliminating even a few of the worse food culprits will help children.) The Web site includes scientific research, testimonials, a list of symptoms, materials available, a newsletter, and resource links.

Greene, A., "Sleep Deprivation and ADHD"
http://www.drgreene.com/21_621.html

This Web site, hosted by Dr. Alan Greene, provides a wealth of good information and a list of research studies linking sleep deprivation and ADD. Greene is on the clinical faculty at Stanford University and president of Health Internet Ethics.

An excerpt from the site: "We know, based on common sense, that inadequate sleep makes kids more moody, more impulsive, and less able to concentrate. . . . Recent research has verified that chronic poor sleep results in daytime tiredness, difficulties with focused attention, low threshold to express negative emotion (irritability and easy frustration), and difficulty modulating impulses and emotions. . . . These are the same symptoms that can earn kids the diagnosis of attention deficit hyperactivity."

Living Well, "Attention Deficit and Hyperactivity"
http://www.thebook.com/livewell/info_add.htm

This site offers recommended readings; assistance in finding a physician who will help with natural alternatives; and information about food and environmental sensitivities, yeast, the effect of specific vitamins and supplements, and side effects of prescription medication.

Dr. Thomas Armstrong
http://www.thomasarmstrong.com

Dr. Thomas Armstrong is the author of several books, including *The Myth of the A.D.D. Child: Fifty Ways to Improve Your Child's Behavior and Attention Span Without Drugs, Labels, or Coercion* (Plume, 1997). I was impressed with his argument that the current diagnoses for ADD-ADHD are too often simplistic and negative. I was further impressed that he makes two chapters of his book *ADD/ADHD Alternatives in the Classroom* available to read on-line, which leads me to believe that he is more concerned with helping children than with selling books. My kind of guy. Check out chapters titled "Limitations and Assumptions of the ADHD Paradigm" and "Strategies to Empower, Not Control, Kids Labeled ADD/ADHD."

The Gift of ADHD
http://www.thomhartmann.com/home-add.shtml

Thom Hartmann is host of a radio program and the author of eight books on attention deficit disorder, including *ADD: A Different Perception* (Underwood Books, October 1997). He created the metaphor of the hunter in a farmer's world, which suggests that behaviors now unacceptable in the classroom once helped humans survive in a sometimes hostile environment. His theories are thought-provoking. In one article, for example, he suggests that people who are diagnosed as having ADHD require more stimulation than most people do in order to feel alive. Another article explores the differences between the way ADHD is viewed depending on children's gender.

Dr. Mary Ann Block, the Block Center
http://www.blockcenter.com

Author of *No More Ritalin* (Kensington Books, 1996), Dr. Block is a licensed osteopathic physician who entered medical school when traditional treatments failed to heal her own child. Block's method is based on the belief that treating the symptoms won't cure the problem. She focuses on underlying causes of ADD-ADHD such as hypoglycemia, allergies, environmental factors, and hyperthyroidism. She provides case histories, sets dietary guidelines, gives a good list of resources, and explains how to enhance the learning process. Block has developed a series of programs and materials people can purchase for use at home.

Death from Ritalin: The Truth Behind ADHD
http://www.ritalindeath.com/packageinsert.htm

This Web site reproduces an insert from a Ritalin prescription—pretty scary reading. The Web site name seems a little melodramatic until you learn on the home page that it was created by a couple whose young son died after taking Ritalin. They include the date of death, the doctor's name, and this statement from their son's death certificate: "Death caused from Long Term Use of Methylphenidate, (Ritalin)." They list a number of important items of information that they believe are being withheld from parents who must decide whether to medicate their children. It is worth a quick read, at least.

Psychiatric Drug Facts
http://www.breggin.com

Dr. Peter R. Breggin, author of *Talking Back to Ritalin* (1998; revised edition, Perseus, 2001) is one of the most outspoken, well-educated, and articulate opponents to the use of Ritalin and other stimulants for ADD-ADHD. Breggin has been a practicing psychiatrist for over thirty years (his subspecialty is clinical psychopharmacology) and has written dozens of scientific articles and books.

This Web site has an extensive index of articles—some very scientific, all well documented. Find information here about Prozac, Paxil, neuroleptics, stimulant side effects, jury verdicts in cases involving pharmacology, congressional investigations into Ritalin and ADHD, and so on. Dr. Breggin also provides the address and phone number of his New York office.

12

My Dream School

Occasionally, I fantasize about taking a vacation to a tropical beach during the winter months; and quite often I fantasize about eating some decadently delicious chocolate mousse. But my favorite and most frequent fantasy involves creating the perfect school. If Bill Gates or Donald Trump or Arnold Schwarzenegger would just send me the money, I know I could build a school where every child would learn, a school where "no child left behind" would be a reality and not a catchy campaign slogan or an impossible dream.

My dream of designing the perfect school started when I taught kids who hated school. The school system labeled those kids as being at risk. After working with them for a few years, I labeled them disenchanted, which is a much more appropriate adjective in my opinion. In fact, adjective revision is one of the first things on my agenda for creating a great school. The following adjectives, commonly found in public schools, will no longer be authorized for use in describing students: *at risk, apathetic, hyperactive, retarded, unmotivated, lazy, unteachable,* and *dumb.* Instead, we'll use the following more accurate adjectives: *frightened, angry, confused, bewildered, abused, undernourished, sleep-deprived, poverty-stricken, unhealthy, illiterate, hopeless, intimidated, ill-educated, ignored,* and *forgotten.* Occasionally, a student will turn out to be a true little stinker, but most will not. Applying the proper adjectives from the beginning will enable us to solve many of the problems that plague our schools without resorting to threats, punishment, expulsions, pharmaceuticals, or lawsuits.

In addition to banishing inappropriate adjectives, my dream school design begins with the abandonment of three basic assumptions that are the root of many educational evils. The following beliefs are forthwith expunged:

1. Students must be divided equally among teachers.

2. Punishment creates long-term changes in behavior.

3. Students must be grouped by age, regardless of differences in ability, rates of mental development, and time required to process new information.

Without those slow and ponderous ideas (which have everything to do with ease of administration and nothing to do with children's needs) holding back our brains, we are now free to entertain new and more effective ideas such as those that my former disenchanted, hopeless, angry students offered (many of whom went on to college and excellent jobs such as designing video games and producing television shows). One of my students' favorite journal-writing assignments was to demolish the current public school system and articulately describe its replacement. After much writing, reading, debate, and discussion, they concocted a pretty darned good design for a new school, Totally Cool School (TCS). My dream school is built on the TCS foundation that those talented and successful unteachable students outlined, but my design also incorporates elements from my own research, reading, experience, and conversations with teachers from around the world.

And now please join me for a tour of the new, improved TCS. You will notice immediately that our building is far more attractive than most of the public schools being built today. Instead of featuring the prison look, with many windowless walls and an uninviting facade, TCS is a beautiful redbrick building with a low-maintenance but attractive little park in front. There are benches beneath shady trees where people can sit comfortably when they need to wait for somebody. Flowering hedges surround a hopscotch sidewalk, water fountains, trash cans, and bicycle racks. Squirrel-proof bird feeders hang from the trees, and small beds of wild flowers dot the grounds.

Students maintain this entrance park, earning credit for horticulture and landscape studies under the direction of trained botanists or landscape architects. Because students are responsible for maintaining the park, they police themselves—and others—to ensure that littering and vandalism don't damage their beloved school yards.

The TCS campus consists of a series of buildings arranged in an oval shape, surrounding a big central courtyard and park. The entire campus is fenced with wood, stone, stucco, or concrete—something tall enough to provide security from intruders and prevent people from passing anything over, under, or through the fence into the school yard. Adult community volunteers constantly police the perimeter of the campus and report any suspicious activity to the school Student Safety office, which also maintains security cameras such as those found in twenty-four-hour convenience stores. Emergency fire exits are placed throughout the school, but open only from the inside and are monitored at all times by closed-circuit cameras and Student Safety personnel.

Students, school staff, and visitors all enter and exit through the TCS main entrance, located directly in front of the principal's office and Student Safety headquarters. Every student, teacher, administrator, and staff member has an ID card containing a hologram and signature. Without the ID card, nobody is permitted to enter the school building until Student Safety has verified their identity. Everybody, including Student Safety personnel, passes through a metal detector on the way into the school; and an armed guard monitors the entrance—not just to deter pedophiles, pornographers, and assorted lunatics but so that students in this school do not have to worry about weapons on campus.

Let me interrupt our tour for a moment to share an important aside. I am not a paranoid, crabby old lady who shakes her gray head at the decline of civilization. Well, perhaps I do shake my head and sigh. And I do suffer from nostalgia about my own school days, back when the really bad boys drank a beer or sneaked a cigarette behind the bleachers at a football game and a black eye was about the worse damage one student might do to another. But the emphasis on school security is based on real life. We live in a dangerous world, and children acknowledge that fact, even when adults refuse to give up the illusion that children's school years are a carefree time. For six years I taught children who lived in gang-ridden, violence-plagued neighborhoods. One of their chief concerns was safety. Many of them simply couldn't sit still and concentrate on their lessons because they felt they needed to be on guard against assault from outside our classroom. When we drafted an emergency response plan, locked the door, covered the windows with construction paper, and posted a "guard" near the door to our classroom, those students were able to sit down and learn.

Those scared students weren't paranoid or overly suspicious. They were reacting normally to a stressful environment. Researchers across the country, many inspired by the 1999 Columbine High School shootings, have concluded that danger and stress can inhibit certain kinds of thinking and memory, making it difficult for students to succeed in schools where they don't feel safe. Professor W. Thomas Boyce at University of California Berkeley studies the impact of stress on children, and he maintains that children who fear for their safety cannot learn as well as children who feel safe and nurtured. Professor Boyce's research coincides with that of Dr. David Sousa, who urges teachers to move past the outdated idea that teachers should ignore emotion and focus solely on intellect. Dr. Sousa has written several books about the way the brain learns, and he stresses the important role emotion plays in the ability and desire to learn. He believes that the way students feel about their school environment has a great deal to do with how well they learn in that environment. Thus, TCS will be an educational haven where children can relax and concentrate on learning.

Some people have said to me, "You cannot make a school secure." I beg to differ. Banks, jewelry stores, legal firms, and a plethora of other businesses and buildings enforce security by various means. Therefore, I maintain that if we care for our children as much as we do our money and our material valuables, we can take the same effective measures to protect them and their school grounds. We post closed-circuit cameras, install silent alarms, and maintain a twenty-four-hour immediate-response security service. We also institute an active neighborhood watch program, whereby people who live near the schools keep an eye on the campus.

Oh, yes, I know. Some parents will protest having a closed campus because they want immediate access to their children. But their children do not have immediate access to them when they are at work because immediate access makes it too easy for those who shouldn't have access at all. TCS is a closed campus because that is the best way to ensure the safety of the children and their safety is my number one priority. Their safety takes priority over parents' desire to have quick and convenient access to the school grounds. Like all visitors, parents will have to pass through the Student Safety checkpoint and show proper ID before being admitted to the campus. But parents will be welcome to attend classes whenever they wish, except during major exam periods when their presence may disrupt students.

"What about food?" some parents will ask. "If my student has to stay on campus, how can I be sure he or she will get a decent lunch? Or breakfast? Or after-school snack? My kids hate cafeteria food and so do I."

I also hate traditional cafeteria food—macaroni and cheese casseroles and lime Jell-O. There will be no such foods at TCS because we acknowledge that young bodies need proper fuel if we expect the young heads attached to those bodies to function effectively. TCS will not sell student health to the highest bidder, even if those bidders offer billion-dollar bribes. TCS has no soda franchises, candy company contracts, or burger vendors. Our food is free of chemical preservatives and additives, artificial coloring and dyes, artificial sweeteners, and trans-fats because those substances have proved, time and again, to cause allergies and health problems. Foods are organic and free of genetically modified ingredients. Free-range chicken nuggets prepared with unbleached flour and olive oil are just as tasty as salmonella-plagued chicken dredged in bleached flour and soaked in saturated fat. Our menu includes obviously healthy choices such as veggie and turkey burgers, yogurt, granola, fresh vegetable and fruit juices, crackers and cookies, fresh salads and fruits, dried fruits and nuts, chocolate soy milk, fruit smoothies, and raw veggies with dip. We also offer organic, whole-grain versions of favorites such as pizza, nachos, chips and dips—but they do not contain hydrogenated oils, artificial sweeteners, bleached flours, and preservatives whose names most of us can't pronounce.

Our staff nutritionist provides written information for parents who may not know how food affects their children's moods, behavior, health, and brain function. Our nutritionist also offers evening classes for parents and community members who want to learn about specific diets that have proved to be successful in eliminating attention deficit hyperactivity disorder symptoms in many children. Because all vitamins are not created equal, students who attend TCS nutrition classes receive guidance and information to help them choose high-quality vitamin and mineral supplements. We don't want our parents to fall prey to unscrupulous manufacturers who may try to take advantage of their desperate desire to help their children excel in school.

It is early morning, thirty minutes before school begins, but the cafeteria lounge is filled with students who are sipping hot chocolate and orange juice, playing chess or checkers or Scrabble at one of the small tables along the walls. Soft background music—classical or jazz—provides inspiration for the students in the far corner who are using the yoga mats to stretch and perform a few simple exercises before heading off to class.

Outside the cafeteria window, we see other students in the central park, playing basketball, skipping rope, walking on the gravel path that winds among the trees and shrubs, sitting on wooden benches to watch the birds and squirrels. Oops! Two girls argue over a basketball move. "That's cheating," one girl insists. "No, it isn't," says the other. "You just don't know how to play." They begin to tussle. Suddenly, a shrill whistle pierces the air. All of the students in the park turn their attention to the two girls. The boy who blew the whistle (every TCS student carries a whistle) shakes his head and reminds his schoolmates that fighting and name calling are not acceptable at TCS. If the girls can't come to an agreement, they must agree not to play basketball together any longer. If they continue to fight, they will be barred from using the park for a period of time to be determined by the Peer Council. The girls decide to give up the game and find something else to do. Perhaps they will play again tomorrow when they have had time to cool down.

From her post nearby, a TCS park ranger (one of many adult volunteers from local businesses who donate an hour of their time to the school during their workday) watches to make sure that the argument doesn't escalate into a fight. She has already alerted security to the possibility that assistance may be required. They will give the girls a few minutes to work out their problem because TCS students know they must accept responsibility for their own behavior. If either girl had struck the other, our park ranger would have intervened within seconds. In addition to a whistle and a radio, she also carries a stun gun—something she has never had to use because all TCS students attend conflict resolution classes at the beginning of each school year. They learn how to solve problems, argue reasonably, listen effectively, and cool down when they are feeling too hot to handle. (Many students take the conflict resolution course materials home and leave them on the kitchen counter, where they hope their parents will read them.)

Our park ranger advises Student Safety that the conflict is no longer a threat. She provides the names of the two girls, however, so that a counselor can contact them during the day to make sure neither of them is harboring a grudge that might result in plans for revenge. The park ranger knows the names of nearly all the students at TCS. Our school isn't a huge school. It is smaller than

many modern schools. We have a maximum of 750 students, ranging in age from six to eighteen. We don't believe it is effective, ethical, or humane to merge several schools and make students travel
several miles from their homes. Bigger schools often qualify for bigger funding, but bigger isn't always better for children, who need to
feel special and unique while they are young. Many children act
out because they want to be noticed. They need adult attention,
and at TCS they get it. We are a small neighborhood school where
children can walk, ride their bikes, or skate their way to us in the
mornings. If at some future date we should have more students than
we have desks, we will not put a trailer in the backyard. We will
build another school. If population changes in the future bring
declining enrollments, then we will use our existing schools as
community centers where we will offer enrichment classes, GED,
adult basic education, literacy services, tutoring, after-school programs, preschool, and preparation for tests such as the SAT. We
will train people in the community to write grants so that they can
get money to fund the other programs at our school location.

Now let's enter the front door of the administration building at
TCS. We pass through Student Safety and wave to the principal,
who is waiting in the lobby to greet students as they arrive in the
morning. She (or he) is usually surrounded by students who have a
question, comment, or suggestion to offer to their principal, who
actually listens to them. This principal also teaches class for one
hour per day, alternating grades each day so that he or she knows
exactly what challenges and obstacles face the students at TCS.

In addition to the principal's office, the administration building contains the guidance office; a medical clinic with two licensed
physicians, one traditional and one holistic; the college advisement
center where students attend SAT preparation and apply for financial aid; a school-to-job-center that arranges and monitors students
with jobs at local companies; and a day care center for infants of
both students and staff, operated by students who plan to become
teachers and business leaders (payment is based on a sliding scale).
In addition, the building contains the Peer Council conference

room and the Opportunity Center—two areas that are not likely to be familiar because I made them up.

The Peer Council conference room contains two large conference tables surrounded by executive padded leather chairs and a courtroom complete with judge's bench, jury seating, and witness box. The Peer Council is composed of randomly selected students with a rotating membership. Peer Council members serve as jury members, judges, or attorneys for the prosecution and defense. At any given time, the council will include three judges, ten jury members, and two attorneys. (Students who commit violent acts, misdemeanors, or felonies are barred from serving on the Peer Council for one year, after which time the current council can reinstate them.) The Peer Council reviews all violations of the TCS student conduct code (a joint effort of the Peer Council and the school staff), and its judgments are legal, final, and binding. The council can assign a range of consequences from written letters of apology to community service to permanent expulsion from school. In the case of crimes that fall under the jurisdiction of local or federal authorities, the Peer Council still reviews the case and recommends sentencing and consequences in addition to those that the juvenile justice system may assign.

The Opportunity Center replaces the traditional detention center and disciplinary office. The Opportunity Center provides students with an opportunity to consider their behavior, adjust their attitudes, and receive help for whatever obstacles are keeping them from being successful in school. When a teacher sends a student out of the classroom for inappropriate behavior—whether it's daydreaming, disrupting class, destroying school property, persisting in being tardy, sleeping, refusing to cooperate, and so on—the teacher writes a brief description of the situation and sends the student directly to the Opportunity Center.

The Opportunity Center staff includes two current members of the Peer Council jury along with two licensed psychologists and two licensed therapists who are experts in family and child counseling. When a student enters the Opportunity Center the first stop is the

Peer Council desk, where the student must state his or her problem or situation in writing. The Peer Council then sets a date to review the case and assign any appropriate consequences. If the offense is serious and requires legal action, the student then goes directly to the principal's office for further action. If the offense does not require legal action, the Peer Council members discuss the situation with the student and the council members either send the student back to class or refer the student to one of the adult counselors. Students who are referred to adult counselors are interviewed and either sent back to class or enrolled in one of the following programs: anger management and conflict resolution, individual counseling, martial arts, art therapy, dance or exercise class, weight training, yoga, ROTC, or accelerated or remedial reading classes. (Yes, these programs cost money, but they will still be far cheaper—and more beneficial to society—than juvenile detention centers and prisons.)

Students who are referred to the Opportunity Center more than once are automatically enrolled in the program that is most likely to meet their individual needs. If the counselors determine that the student's problem arises from improper nutrition, food allergies, or lack of sleep, they contact parents or guardians to request their cooperation in addressing the problem. Families who cannot afford counseling or proper nutrition will receive support from a fund endowed by local businesses.

TCS does not have an attendance office. Attendance records are automatically maintained by the computerized hologram ID card at Student Safety, which all students use as they enter and leave the school by the main entrance. We don't waste valuable time, money, or resources hunting down students who don't want to go to school or creating elaborate programs to punish them. Instead, we encourage good attendance by making our school a place where students want to be. Government funding is not contingent on students being present. Just like colleges, TCS requires students to spend a minimum number of hours in class in order to earn credit toward graduation. Teachers provide a syllabus and course outline that clearly state the requirements for passing a course and the number of points students can earn for attendance, assignments, projects, and exams. Students who miss more than the maximum number of class hours receive an incomplete grade and must retake the course. (Because students are not adults, TCS notifies their parents or guardians if students skip so many classes that their grades begin to suffer.)

Because states have their own legal requirements, TCS will provide attendance reports to the appropriate law enforcement agencies. Should those agencies decide that a student is truant, they can take whatever legal action they deem appropriate, at their own expense. TCS is not in the business of rounding up students or taking parents to court. Our job is to educate the students who come to school. Actually, attendance is not a problem at TCS because our students enjoy coming to school.

Enough philosophizing. We have a school to visit. As we leave the administration building and enter one of the classroom buildings, we find ourselves in a wide, well-lighted corridor where colorful and interesting student murals adorn the walls. Huge group photos of students smile at us as we pass by. No industrial gray or green painted surfaces dampen the spirits here. Our floors are hardwood or nicely patterned linoleum (not black and white squares or ugly speckled gray). Our walls are a soothing beautiful blue in locations where we want students to feel calm and peachy and perky or sunny yellow in classrooms where we want students to be awake and alert. And although we repaint the walls every few years to keep them fresh, there is no lingering odor of noxious fumes. We use environmentally friendly clay-based paints that give off no fumes and help regulate room temperature.

Here comes a group of students who are wearing bright red vests and carrying two-way radios. These are our Cool Kids, students with high grade-point averages who are earning community service credits for patrolling the halls of TCS. Cool Kids do not issue orders or challenges to students. They simply observe and report any problems to Student Safety on their two-way radios. Because TCS is a small school and Cool Kids are among the oldest students on campus, they enjoy something of a reputation among their peers. Selection to serve as a Cool Kid is considered a high honor, and students who apply must have the recommendations of at least four teachers. When there are more volunteers than Cool Kid positions, as there usually are, Cool Kids are selected by lottery and their term lasts for one quarter or one semester so that everybody who qualifies gets a chance to serve.

Cool Kids are not police officers. Their job is to monitor. In addition to alerting Student Safety to potential problems, Cool Kids also help students who have forgotten the combinations to the locks on their hall lockers, need change for the pay phone in the cafeteria lounge, or may have dropped an important assignment on the way to class. Cool Kids can issue a bulletin to other monitors for help in locating lost items. Because Cool Kids are on duty throughout the school day, and "Respect yourself and others" is always the order of the day, bullying is not a problem in the TCS hallways and classrooms.

Let's take a quick peek into a classroom. Oh my. It feels light and airy. That's because we don't have any fluorescent lighting to turn us green or flicker and glare on our textbooks so that our eyes hurt and we resist reading. Big windows welcome the sun into the room, and the windows have heavy-duty screens so we can open the windows and enjoy fresh air in the spring when the birds are singing and the blossoms are budding. Regardless of the season and the weather, teachers allow the outside world to distract our students for a few minutes before they sit down to study because they know that students are children who learn as much from watching the world as they do from listening to us lecture them about it.

Before students sit down in their padded chairs (standard molded plastic or plain wooden school chairs are hard on both bottoms and bones), their teacher encourages them to stretch their arms and legs, jump around, make a little noise, and take several deep breaths. Hmm, nice.

The air in our school doesn't smell like industrial cleaning supplies or musty old books. Our school smells clean, with a slight citrus scent because we use nontoxic orange oil–based cleansers, and we have good air purifiers on duty, cleaning the air and preventing the spread of respiratory ailments. Ceiling fans in every room circulate our clean air and cut back on our heating and cooling costs.

In the further interest of keeping TCS students healthy, every bathroom on site has hot and cold running water, antibacterial soap, and air dryers to help prevent the spread of colds and flu. Also, alcohol-based hand cleaners like those used in hospitals are available for people who are in a hurry. A little nook in the back of every bathroom contains a couch and a chair for people who need to escape for a few minutes, perhaps lie down and take a few deep breaths before facing whatever difficulty threatens to overwhelm them. You will notice on the way out, if you didn't on the way in, that a closed-circuit camera is posted near the restroom entrance. Student Safety maintains a record of who goes in and out of every restroom during the day—not because we don't trust our students, but because we want to protect them from harm.

Perhaps you have noticed that some classrooms have twenty students and others have ten or fifteen. That's because progress at TCS is based on practical factors and self-paced exams. After a student has mastered prealgebra, for example, and completed the necessary coursework, she notifies the teacher that she is ready to schedule her exam. If she receives a passing grade, she moves to the next level. Students who complete all the levels in a certain subject area (math, science, English, and so on) may then enroll in correspondence courses, volunteer to act as a peer tutor in the Study Center choose from a number of elective courses, or work on a community service project.

Basic academic subjects take priority at TCS: reading, writing, mathematics, science, history, fine arts, and physical fitness. But every TCS student also learns at least one foreign language because doing so fosters compassion. Our students know firsthand how difficult it is to learn another language, so they are more compassionate when they meet people who are learning to speak English. Also, our students are better prepared to attend college, take advantage of overseas study opportunities, and compete for jobs in the international business community. We also offer a wide range of electives at TCS, including psychology, media studies, journalism, and community service. When a student expresses interest in a subject for which none of our teachers is trained, we find an online computer course or a correspondence course for that student.

Teachers at TCS do not "cover curriculum." They have textbooks, and they teach lessons based on district and state requirements so that students master the necessary skills. Teachers also help students prepare for standardized exams (more about this sore subject later). But a TCS teacher does not arbitrarily design a course of study and then force all students in a given class to learn at the same rate or in the same manner. Instead, teachers schedule a number of lesson or lecture days during which all students participate in the agenda; a lesson may last ten minutes or ten days for a major project. Other days students work on whatever skills they need to master in a given subject. One student may work on grammar exercises, for example, while a small group reads and analyzes a short story. The teacher does not spend his or her time trying to make students hurry up or slow down. Students are not required to spend a semester or a year in any specific grade level. Once they have learned the material, completed the coursework, demonstrated their ability to apply the information, and passed the final exam, students are free to move on. Some students finish freshman English in three months; others may require two years. Those same students, however, may require one year and five months, respectively, in a different subject area, such as science or mathematics.

Because students learn what they need to learn as they need to learn it, teachers do not have to spend several hours each week constructing detailed lesson plans showing how they intend to cover all the objectives in the district and state curriculum guidelines.

Instead, teachers post a master list of readings, coursework, projects, and exams for each particular subject. Second-grade English, for example, might include the following requirements: read five chapter books at grade level, write a coherent paragraph summarizing each book, present an oral review of a book, create a visual or manipulative to support the oral review, master a list of one hundred spelling words, write and construct a children's book that teaches the parts of speech, pass the second-grade English exit exam. The teacher will provide lessons and assistance to help children master the skills required to complete the objectives and pass the exam.

All right, you want to know how we handle standardized exams at TCS. We'll pause here for a moment, outside our library (a popular spot that offers a number of overstuffed chairs where students can relax and enjoy a good read under full-spectrum incandescent lighting or, better yet, in the natural light from a bank of floor-to-ceiling windows). We administer the required standardized state tests to our students because we comply with the legal requirements of an accredited school. But we do not spend valuable staff development time training teachers to teach to the test. Nor do we spend valuable student study time teaching them how to pass a particular exam. All of our students are proficient readers (or working toward that end), and all of our teachers stress higher-level thinking skills. We believe that if you teach a student to pass a particular exam, the student will be able to pass that exam (and if the exam is multiple choice and graded by machine, a monkey could pass a certain percent of the time). But if you teach a student to think well, that student can pass any exam.

Further, we do not believe that any standardized testing instrument can accurately and comprehensively test student knowledge and achievement, particularly when the test concerns mastery of higher-level critical thinking skills and complex abstract concepts. At TCS we conduct tests individually, with an oral component so that students must articulate their ideas and knowledge clearly and demonstrate their skills in a given subject area. Let's say we want to test reading comprehension at the ninth-grade level, for example. Instead of providing a fifty-question multiple-choice, fill-in-the-blank, and short-essay exam, our final exam consists of an oral presentation to two teachers. The student briefly summarizes the plot of a given book. Then he or she answers questions from the teachers about literary techniques and devices in the text, such as irony, literary symbolism, and character development. After completing the oral exam satisfactorily (usually fifteen to twenty minutes), the student has two hours in which to develop a thesis and write a literary analysis of the work. Two different teachers then grade the work and award the student a grade based on the average of the oral and written exams. This system tests not only reading comprehension but also grammar, composition, and spelling—and it employs the highest levels of thinking such as analysis, synthesis, and evaluation. Students who do not pass the written portion then attend classes to work on their weak areas before retaking the exam. Naturally, students are concerned (or embarrassed) when they fail part or all of an exam, but TCS does not hold them back or flunk them out of class; and their embarrassment is not public. They receive immediate feedback about their own level of competency and know exactly what they need to learn in order to pass the exam. Cheating isn't an option, and students are graded on their own merit, not placed in competition with other students.

And that's enough about tests. This country spends far too much time discussing tests as it is. Testing has become a huge industry and has created a bureaucratic bloat that will take years to deflate. At TCS we do our part in support of deflation.

And so we now move on past the library to the Study Center. Unlike the library, where people work quietly so that others can concentrate, we hear students in the Study Center asking questions, sharing ideas, and helping each other solve problems from their homework assignments.

Every student at TCS spends at least one hour per day in the Study Center, where adult and peer tutors are available to provide guidance. The Study Center contains a number of private study carrels, large conference tables, and a series of computer workstations with Internet connections (with excellent porn filters installed). Companies such as Dell, IBM, and Apple fund the computer workstations and reap the benefits of free advertising and a tax write-off in exchange for making their civic contribution. Students may work on homework or other assignments individually or in groups. Those who prefer to wear headsets and listen to music as they study can do so as long as those seated nearby cannot hear their music. (The same rule applies in the classrooms. Some students actually learn more easily when they can listen to music. One theory is that the music drowns out distracting background noise and helps them focus on the work at hand. In order to retain headset privileges, however, a student must maintain passing grades in all courses. Students who earn failing grades are not permitted to wear headsets in school until they bring their grades up to par.)

Reading is the primary focus of academic study at TCS. Students who are good readers are good thinkers. And good thinkers are able to learn any subject. Therefore, all TCS students learn to read. Regardless of grade level, students who cannot read well are enrolled in only four courses: reading, citizenship, physical fitness, and study skills. These four courses help the student learn how to behave and maintain a healthy body to support a healthy mind, and they receive as much tutoring as required in order to complete assignments. But the academic focus of struggling students is always reading because students who do not read well suffer in every other class. Reading specialists work with the students to identify the obstacles that prevent students from reading well and offer a variety of options from one-on-one tutoring to software programs designed to teach phonics.

Because obesity and diabetes are epidemic among American children, TCS ensures that every student has an individualized fitness program, just like those designed by personal trainers at gyms and fitness centers. Regardless of their fitness program, all students must spend at least one hour in the morning and thirty minutes in the afternoon engaged in physical activity. (A teacher may, at his or her discretion, send students who disrupt classes to the fitness center or outside to the park to walk a mile or pump some iron until they can calm down and focus on learning.)

The fitness center, funded partially by corporations such as Gold's Gym, offers weight training, aerobics and yoga classes (either with instructors or videotapes that students can play), martial arts instruction, and an Olympic-sized swimming pool. Dance classes alternate between jazz, hip-hop, ballroom, tap, swing, and country. Students who prefer to exercise outdoors may opt to walk or run on the gravel path that follows the perimeter of the school's Central Park.

Central Park, like the entrance park, is maintained by students who earn credits in horticulture and landscape architecture. Central Park is beautiful, and using it is a privilege. Students who damage property or assault other students lose their park privileges for whatever amount of time the Peer Council specifies. The path surrounding the park is a half-mile gravel trail that curves in and out among tall shade trees, so four laps equals two miles. Students may also swing, play tetherball, jump rope, play hopscotch or badminton, or games of their own design in the grassy center area. Four tennis courts with backboards for solo practice are located at one end of the park, and wooden benches and picnic tables are interspersed among the trees.

Over there in the corner, you can see some kids skating in laps around a concave skateboard park. Students must wear helmets, knee and elbow pads, and follow the safety rules in order to retain their skating privileges. A nonprofit organization operates and maintains the skateboard park, monitoring students and making sure their parents have signed permission slips and insurance waivers that allow them to skate at school. Students may skate between buildings on designated skate paths, but there is no skating in hallways for safety reasons.

Classes are not age-based at TCS, and teachers are not bound by a set curriculum that may or may not address students' needs. Twenty is the maximum number of students in any classroom at a given time. The campus opens to students at 7:00 A.M.; and students are welcome to use the fitness facilities, Central Park, Study Center, cafeteria, and the library before classes begin. The campus remains open to students and staff until 6:00 P.M., at which time almost everything closes. Only the community classroom building remains open for evening courses; parents and students can learn about a variety of topics ranging from nutrition to adolescent psychology to parenting skills.

On the last Friday and Saturday evening of each month, TCS invites the public to attend music concerts, theater presentations, talent shows, art shows, and documentary films—all starring or created by students from TCS—in the campus auditorium. On the other weekends, the school invites TCS students and their families to the auditorium to watch documentaries, educational programs, or other noncommercial and nonviolent movies. Admission and popcorn are free on these family nights because volunteers operate the projectors and concessions.

Quarterly awards ceremonies are held in the auditorium to recognize students who display good citizenship, achieve scholastic honors, produce exceptional science or art projects, maintain perfect attendance at school, and go the entire term without failing a class or receiving any referrals to the Opportunity Center due to inappropriate behavior. Community businesses donate gifts and door prizes for these award ceremonies, and the principal distributes certificates of merit to all award recipients.

Our many activities such as movies, talent shows, after-school classes, and so on do not conflict with sporting events because TCS does not sponsor athletic teams to compete against other schools. The TCS community views sports not as career opportunities but as learning opportunities; games teach teamwork, self-discipline, and coordination and offer children a chance to enjoy themselves in friendly competition. Coed teams play intramural games during fitness classes, but students do not have to try out for teams; everybody who wants to play gets a turn to play. TCS encourages students who prefer a more competitive atmosphere to join community teams, and it allows them to earn physical fitness credits for participating in community activities such as golf, tennis, martial arts, football, basketball, and Little League baseball. TCS students who wish to pursue careers as professional athletes are connected with adult mentors from the local community who have experience playing a particular sport and can provide advice and guidance for our young athletes. Students who demonstrate a clearly exceptional talent for a particular sport may apply for sponsorship from TCS to participate in a rigorous training program to prepare them to compete at the college level, but those students truly are an exception. No student leaves TCS better able to dribble a basketball than to articulate his or her own well-developed critical thinking skills.

Athletic mentors are not the only mentors associated with TCS. We have a large and active pool of volunteers in our Mentor Match program, and we are especially proud and grateful to have them. We match every student who signs up for our program with an adult volunteer whom our mentor advisor has carefully screened. Volunteer mentors come from all walks of life and include retired businesspeople, community college students, homemakers, welders, auto mechanics, and bank presidents. Mentors spend at least one hour per week with students, demonstrating true leadership by their own examples and encouraging young people to stay in school, earn good grades, and contribute to their community.

Not all students sign up for mentors, but every TCS student does sign up for music or art classes and is encouraged to try a variety of instruments and creative tools. Instead of being required to draw a chair or a box, for example, students are free to create their own art; their products are appreciated but not graded. Art instructors teach students about color, design, form, and theory; and they introduce students to classic artists and traditional methods. Music instructors provide a background in music theory, composition, and world-class musicians; but they also encourage students to "toodle around" with different instruments until they find one that plays their particular tune. Art and music at TCS are appreciated, shared, enjoyed, and valued for the important role they play in people's lives as a means of self-expression, creativity, and—in some cases—commercial success.

Now you've had the quick tour of TCS. Yes, it does seem too good to be true. But then again, it isn't impossible or unreasonable to believe that such a school could exist. In fact, I'd like to attend TCS myself. Wouldn't you?

Epilogue:
An Open Letter to Teachers

Dear Teacher,

Thank you.

For continuing to teach in spite of the poor pay, pathetic working conditions, and monumental lack of respect and understanding from the general public about how mentally and emotionally exhausting your job can be.

For taking yet another exam to prove your competence, although you have already completed five years of college and several hundred dollars' worth of standardized tests.

For continuing to teach critical thinking skills and advanced academics in spite of having test after test after test added to your curriculum requirements, without any additional instruction time.

For getting up at 5 or 6 A.M. every day to go to work in a dilapidated trailer or a windowless closet, often with malfunctioning or nonexistent air conditioning and heating.

For eating your lunch out of a paper bag on a folding chair in a sparsely furnished lounge where a working coffeemaker is a treat and a functioning microwave oven is a real luxury.

For spending your so-called time off grading papers; making lesson plans; and attending professional development conferences, committee meetings, restructuring meetings, parent-teaching conferences, school board meetings, and continuing education classes.

For working countless hours of unpaid overtime because it is the only way to do your job well and because you cannot do less. And for not reminding people constantly that if you were paid for your overtime, you could retire tomorrow and never have to work again.

For consistently giving respect to children who don't know what to do with it and don't realize what a valuable gift you are offering.

For caring about children whose own families don't care or don't know how to show that they do.

For spending your own money on pens and pencils, erasers and chalk, paper, tissues, bandages, birthday gifts, treats, clothing, shoes, eyeglasses—and a hundred other things that your students need and don't have.

For spending sleepless nights worrying about a struggling student, wondering what else you might do to help overcome the obstacles that life has placed in his or her path.

For raiding your own children's closets to find a pair of shoes or a sweater for a child who has none.

For putting your own family on hold while you meet with the family of a struggling student.

For believing in the life-changing power of education.

For maintaining your belief that all students can learn if we can learn how to teach them.

For putting up with the aching back, sore knees, tired legs, and exhausted feet that go with the teaching territory.

For giving hopeless children enough hope to continue struggling against the poverty, prejudice, abuse, alcoholism, hunger, and apathy that are a daily part of so many tender young lives.

For risking your job to give a child a much-needed hug.

For biting your tongue and counting to a million while a parent lists the reasons why your incompetence is responsible for the misbehavior of his or her undisciplined, spoiled, or obnoxious child.

For taking on the most difficult, challenging, frustrating, emotionally exhausting, mentally draining, satisfying, wonderful, precious job in the world.

You are truly an unsung American hero.

With respect and gratitude,
LouAnne Johnson

Appendix:
Two-Minute Reviews

This is not an exhaustive or definitive list of resources. Rather, these are short reviews of Web sites, books, and other resources about teaching, children, and human behavior that I find thought-provoking or informative. They might be of interest to people who are concerned about the health, well-being, and education of our children.

Web Sites

About Discipline.com
http://www.aboutdiscipline.com

Marvin Marshall's Web site is clearly a commercial enterprise, but it provides enough good information at no charge to make it worthwhile. Marshall is the author of Phi Delta Kappa's "Fostering Social Responsibility" program and the book *Discipline Without Stress, Punishments or Rewards: How Teachers and Parents Promote Responsibility* (Piper Press, 2001).

Some of his articles on promoting responsibility are available in PDF format, including "Tips for Parents"—a one-page cram course in how to talk and listen to your child effectively. A former teacher, counselor, and principal, Marshall now writes and conducts staff development and seminars using his three-step strategy for teaching children how to be responsible.

African-American Unschooling
http://www.afamunschool.com

This Africentric homeschooling Web site is hosted by S. Courtney Walton, author of the "Real Living . . . Real Learning" column in the *St. Louis Good News Herald*. Walton is founder of African-American Unschoolers, which seeks to provide networking opportunities, ideas, articles, general information for homeschoolers, and links to resources that positively reflect African and African American culture.

This Web site is well maintained and includes a wide spectrum of information, resources, and links—from African paper dolls to an Egyptian language and culture course from Temple University. You'll find links to the *Internet Living Swahili Dictionary*; information about Buffalo Soldiers, black cowboys, and the Underground Railroad; daily news from the African continent; and a great selection of books that might otherwise escape notice or be difficult to find. The site also offers two support groups for parents and teens, an e-zine, and a DVD rental service for homeschoolers.

Bordessa, K. "Reading and Perpetual Motion." *Home Education Magazine,* **Nov.-Dec. 2003.**
http://www.home-ed-magazine.com/HEM/206/ndread.html
Kris Bordessa describes her struggle to teach her two very different sons to read: one loves to sit quietly and read, while the other needs to move and talk. At first she tried to make her lively child "turn it off" before she realized that he couldn't. "Evan's apparent inattention and seeming disinterest was so blatant that I neglected to see this as his own style of learning," Bordessa writes. She then explains how she learned to teach Evan effectively. Parents and teachers will be able to relate to her efforts to accommodate both boys and might get some new ideas for working with their own energetic young readers.

Born to Explore! The Other Side of ADD
http://www.borntoexplore.org
This Web site proposes to explore the other side of ADD and contains a good range of resources, information about nutrition and

ADD, plus a lot of links to further information. Teresa Gallagher, an environmental scientist who homeschools her two children, maintains the site. She posts information "about creativity, learning styles and giftedness to counter the idea that all those kids labeled with attention deficit disorder actually have something wrong with them." This site presents nutritional and scientific information in everyday language and provides links to an array of resources, book reviews, inspirational quotations, articles, and essays (including one entitled "The Problem with CHADD" that provides one of the more balanced critiques of the organization).

Brain Connection
http://www.brainconnection.com

Make sure you have some time when you visit this Web site because you will want to stay and play while you learn. Brain Connection claims to offer "brain science in plain English," and it delivers. Editors and contributing writers include scientists, researchers, and professors with expertise in areas such as brain plasticity, integrative neuroscience, language-learning disabilities, behavioral algorithms and psychophysics, English literature, and creative writing.

From the home page, you can choose tabs to visit subpages: education connection, library, brain teasers, conferences, marketplace, or professional development. The library section is my favorite, with articles and information on a range of subjects from basic child development and reading fundamentals to autism and ADD. From the library you can click on one of four buttons: talk, play, explore, or review. The talk button takes you to columns and interviews. Play goes to games that tickle the brain or test reading and language skills. Explore offers "Brain Basics" (a tutorial on the central nervous system's anatomy, physiology, and function), along with animations that demonstrate what happens in your brain when you read, hear, or speak a word; images and illustrations that are perfect for teaching students; on-line courses to improve your understanding and increase your effectiveness as a teacher; and an assortment of brain facts (for example, the average human brain weighs three pounds). I love this Web site because it proves that learning—even about a complex subject—can be entertaining and exciting.

http://www.disciplinehelp.com

For parents and teachers who struggle with discipline, the You Can Handle Them All discipline model offers free advice as well as books and videotapes. You can select the link "Solutions for Handling 117 Behaviors" and then choose from a long list of problem behaviors from the agitator to the whiner. When you select a behavior, the page displays suggested actions for teachers or parents and gives common mistakes that adults make when they want to change children's behavior. The discussion section has questions and answers for parents who are seeking help in handling their children—not a lot of responses to some questions, but the ones that are available have some good advice. Sometimes just knowing somebody else faces the same problem makes it a little easier to handle.

Drazen, J. M., M.D. "Institutions, Contracts, and Academic Freedom" (editorial). *New England Journal of Medicine,* 2002, *347*(17), 1362–1363.
http://content.nejm.org/cgi/content/full/347/17/1362

This editorial from the *New England Medical Journal* concerns the increasing concern that many research scientists are funded and then pressured by pharmaceutical companies to produce results that please the companies or risk not having the results of their research published. In the case of controversial substances such as aspartame and methylphenidate, biased research or reports could be very harmful to children. A Duke University study of research contracts found that less than 1 percent of the contracts guaranteed that results would be published and only 1 percent of contracts required an independent board to monitor patient safety.

The journal's home page (http://content.nejm.org) allows on-line users to access back issues free of charge six months after an article's publication. This is a good source for current information on medical topics that the mainstream commercial media may ignore or condense to a one-paragraph filler or ten-second sound bite.

Fielding, R. "Lighting the Learning Environment."
http://www.designshare.com/Research/Lighting/Lighting
        Envr1.htm. 2000

This article is a scientific yet very readable discussion about lighting classrooms for the best comfort and efficiency. Fielding explains why full-spectrum lighting has become so popular, without all the hype you'll find if you go to a commercial Web site. I don't have enough expertise to make a recommendation about buying a particular brand of lights, but I would recommend switching to full-spectrum fluorescents or incandescent lighting when children have problems reading. Many people are sensitive to the flickering, glare, and reduced color spectrum of standard fluorescent lights, which are common in many classrooms—lights chosen purely because they are cheaper, not because they are better for students. Most people find it easier to read in light that is closer to sunlight. Natural sunlight has a color rendering index (CRI) of one hundred (the higher the CRI, the more natural colors appear). Standard cool white incandescent bulbs have a CRI of sixty-four, and full-spectrum bulbs usually have a CRI of ninety or higher.

Johnston, L. "Sweetener Probed." *Sunday Express*, **May 20,**
        2001, p. 7.
http://321recipes.com/sunday_express.html

Johnston provides a collection of links to published articles, studies, personal testimonials, and over fifty doctors' opinions on the dangers of aspartame (marketed as Equal or NutraSweet). If you visit even a few of these sites, I believe you will stop consuming aspartame.

In her introduction to the list of sources, Johnston states: "the FDA denied aspartame approval for over 8 years until the newly appointed FDA commissioner Arthur Hayes overruled the final scientific review panel, approved aspartame, and then went to work for G. D. Searle's (initial owner of aspartame) public relations firm at $1,000 a day. Hayes has refused all interviews to discuss his actions."

I did not read all of the listed references, but I read enough of them (and did further research to verify names and titles) to convince me that nobody should eat or drink anything containing aspartame. Medical doctors, scientists, and independent researchers claim that the sweetener is responsible for an incredible array of health problems from blindness to liver cancer. Many nutritionists believe that aspartame can cause learning problems for children.

Learning Styles Network
http://www.learningstyles.net (Note: This site is accessible only to users of Internet Explorer.)

The home page of the Center for the Study of Learning and Teaching Styles at St. John's University in Jamaica, New York, this Web site highlights the research and learning styles model of Doctors Rita Dunn and Kenneth Dunn. Click on the tab labeled D&D Model to see an illustrated model of stimuli that affect student learning, from environmental sources such as sound and light to physiological elements such as energy levels and need for mobility while learning. The Dunns back this very interesting concept up with a lot of research and practical application.

The Dunns have devoted their lives to studying how children learn and how best to teach them. I remember reading many years ago about their research into why children couldn't focus in school. One of the startling facts they uncovered was that the average plastic or wood school seat places more than 70 percent of the body weight on 4 percent of the child's bones.

National Reading Styles Institute (NRSI)
http://www.nrsi.com

This Web site highlights Marie Carbo's award-winning programs for motivating and helping struggling readers. Both the National Education Association and the National Staff Development Council have positively reviewed Carbo's Reading Styles Program and her recorded books are popular with both teachers and young readers.

I purchased the sample package of overlays just to see how they compared to the Irlen patented filter. Although the samples are small (not large enough to cover even a half page), the color selection is good, and the NRSI overlays seemed to match the Irlen filter's clarity and consistency. The multicolored transparencies I purchased at the local office supply store looked cloudy and irregular in comparison.

Reading Lady.com: Teacher Resource Center
http://www.readinglady.com

For anybody who is trying to teach a young child or an older child who hates reading, this site has a wealth of information, exercises, activities, and inspiration. The Reading Lady is a teacher who uses her own experiences and research to help others. For primary grade teachers, the site provides a professional reading group (restricted membership) that generates a discussion on a different book each month. For the rest of us, there is much more. Four of the many choices are author studies, comprehension, Reader's Theater, and poetry.

Author studies includes tips for making a connection between books and writers in your classroom to inspire kids to read.

Comprehension offers eighteen different options, including step-by-step instruction strategies for a variety of exercises. The Reading Lady incorporates the best practices from a variety of sources and always credits the original source.

Reader's Theater is a big hit with kids of all ages—don't overlook this for older kids. Forty-eight different scripts cover a wide spectrum, from *The True Story of the Three Pigs* to Dom DeLuise's hilarious version of *Hansel and Gretel*.

Teaching poetry might be a piece of cake if you use the material available here. The site groups collections of poetry into eleven categories (bats, dinosaurs, friends, books, and so on) that you can print out, and most suggest some good books for guided poetry reading.

Thomas S. Szasz Cybercenter for Liberty and Responsibility
http://www.szasz.com

People who are intrigued by the concept that mental illness in itself is subjective will enjoy the thought-provoking philosophies of Dr. Thomas Szasz, author of a long list of books and articles ranging from *The Myth of Mental Illness: Foundations of a Theory of Personal Conduct* (Paul B. Hoeber, 1961) to *Pharmacracy: Medicine and Politics in America* (Praeger, 2001). Szasz defines the term *pharmacracy* as "the substitution of medical controls for legal and religious controls." Dr. Szasz's take on the ADD-ADHD controversy is clear: he maintains that ADHD doesn't exist. In one essay he likens the current obsession with controlling children's behavior to another, earlier obsession:

> The disease of masturbation was the favorite diagnosis of doctors and parents dealing with troublesome children in the nineteenth century; attention deficit hyperactivity disorder is the favorite diagnosis of doctors and parents dealing with troublesome children today. Belief in masturbatory insanity was, as I emphasized, not an innocent error. Neither is belief in ADHD. Each belief is a manifestation of the adults' annoyance by certain ordinary childhood activities, their efforts to control or eliminate the activities to allay their own discomfort, and the medical profession's willingness to diagnose disturbing childhood behaviors, thus medicalizing and justifying the domestication of children by drugs defined as therapeutic. Formerly, quacks had fake cures for real diseases; now, they claim to have real cures for fake diseases.

Teachers.Net
http://teachers.net

This is one of the most useful of the thousands of Web sites available for teachers (or homeschooling parents). In the Lesson Bank, you can search, submit, browse, or request lesson plans on virtually any subject or grade level, from preschool to adult education, from English literature to soccer strategies. The bank provides the name and grade level of the teacher who submitted the lesson plan, along with a detailed description for using it in your own classroom. The jobs tab provides an updated list of links to teaching jobs by geographic region.

The tool I find most useful on this site is the chatboard. This site is clearly popular with teachers, based on the number and quality of questions and answers—and occasionally arguments.

You can choose from a number of chatboards by age or occupation (substitute, beginning teacher, adult education instructor), curriculum (English, technology, projects) or general interest. The classroom management and classroom discipline chatboards both have a spirited exchange of information, with some really good suggestions from dynamic teachers. But beware the curmudgeons and complainers. Although sometimes I find myself thinking that some ill-guided teacher has just taught me something *not* to do in my own classroom, those lessons may turn out to be the most valuable.

Books

Amen, D. G. *Healing ADD* (Berkley, 2001).

Parents who don't have time or energy to conduct extensive research for good books about ADD and ADHD may be tempted to give up when they see the stacks of books on the subject at the local library or bookstore. This book is one of the most well balanced and informative I have encountered.

Amen's book takes a more scholarly approach than most, including lots of illustrations and scientific explanations, with pointers to numerous studies for further information. Amen presents a very detailed description of brain activity and categorizes ADD into six different types. Amen warns that a variety of other problems may accompany ADD or may be misdiagnosed as ADD: psychiatric or family problems, depression, manic depression, anxiety, obsessive-compulsive disorder, abuse, medical factors such as birth or head trauma, and learning or developmental idiosyncrasies. He explores a host of interventions including dietary changes, medications, nutritional supplements, neurofeedback, focused breathing, self-hypnosis, parenting and family strategies, and school strategies. He explains how thoughts can affect hand temperature, heart rate, blood pressure, muscle tension, and learning.

One particularly interesting passage in this book discusses an incident that occurred in Japan in 1997 after the television broadcast of a cartoon that contained an explosion accompanied by multicolored flashing lights. That night 730 children were taken to hospital emergency rooms because of brain seizures; most had no previous history of seizures. Amen explains that TV and computer screens flash at rates of up to thirty cycles per second and our brains gravitate to particular rhythms. Slower rates make people sleepy; faster rates make them feel energized or anxious. According to Amen, if your brain tunes in to a "concentration" rate of flashing you will focus on the TV or computer screen—even though you may not be interested in what appears there. Amen suggests that we need to conduct studies to find out the effects on children of long periods of exposure to flashing lights from computers.

Aron, E. *The Highly Sensitive Person: How to Thrive When the World Overwhelms You* (Broadway, 1996).

According to research psychologist Elaine Aron, more than 15 percent of the population is highly sensitive and deeply affected by noise, light, stress, and other people's moods. Aron proposes that highly sensitive people have more activity in the right hemisphere of their brains and are therefore more inwardly oriented and inclined to be shy, anxious, or depressed if they are mistreated as children.

Her book includes a list of excellent suggestions for teachers of highly sensitive students. Some of the suggestions are common sense, but others point out possibilities that might not immediately come to mind (giving a sensitive student the opportunity to perform a dress rehearsal before giving an oral presentation, for example).

An interesting point for teachers: the harder highly sensitive people try when under pressure, the more likely they are to fail. High levels of stimulation (such as a noisy classroom) exhaust them sooner than other students. Some sensitive kids will withdraw, and some will become hyperactive (especially boys).

Aron advises teachers not to assume that a student who is just watching is shy or afraid. Teachers often try to draw out students they perceive as shy, which may cause more problems for the child than simply noting that the child prefers to be quiet and observant.

Berne, S. A. *Without Ritalin* (McGraw-Hill, 2002).

There is no doubt where Dr. Berne stands on the issue of medicating children, but this book isn't a diatribe—it is inspiring and encouraging. Berne intersperses anecdotal case studies with statistics and information from scientific studies. He discusses possible causes for learning problems, from toxins such as pesticides to allergies, sinus infections, yeast problems, sleep deprivation, and vision disorders. He presents an unvarnished description of how different medications work (psychostimulants, antihypertensives, anticonvulsants, and antipsychotics). He recommends finding a health practitioner who is holistic, one who treats the whole child, not simply ADD symptoms.

Two things Berne discusses are missing from many books: an explanation of the stages of normal behavioral development and the idea of performing exercises to promote developmental learning—a series of activities such as upper body swings and deep breathing that are specifically designed to help a child or adult learn sensory-motor and cognitive skills on an automatic, subconscious level. Each chapter of this complex and analytical book contains footnotes and numerous references to other sources of information.

Hubbs, D. *Home Education Resource Guide* (Bluebird Publishing, 1989).

Hubbs begins this handy little book (125 pages) with legal information about homeschooling, followed by lists of resources for correspondence courses, testing and curriculum design, textbooks and supplies, educational toys and games, software, book lists for specific grade levels, magazines, Bible education, how-to books for homeschoolers, help for handicapped children, speakers and seminars, audiovisual materials, music education, a directory of publishers, and a list of support groups and national organizations devoted to providing information for homeschooling families. The section on child training includes pointers to information on character development, Montessori principles, parent-child communication, and discipline.

Holt, J. C. *How Children Fail* (Perseus, 1995) and *How Children Learn* (Perseus, 1995).

The best books ever written about education, in my opinion (and still in print decades after their initial publication), are *How Children Fail* and *How Children Learn*. Extraordinary teacher John Holt kept diaries about his teaching experiences and his ideas are accessible even when they involve complex philosophical questions or psychological theories. Holt's books influenced my own teaching and, I believe, enabled me to successfully teach many students that the school system had designated as unteachable. It was his idea, for example, to grade student journal writing on ideas only, regardless of spelling or grammar, which resulted in much better writing in the long term. Just about any page of any John Holt book will include a thought-provoking passage.

Holt died in 1985, but his family and colleagues collected materials for a work in progress that Addison-Wesley published as *Learning All the Time* (1989).

Independent Study Catalog (**Peterson's Guides, 7th edition, 1998**).

This guide is useful for parents who homeschool; young students in traditional schools who want to supplement their studies or increase their knowledge base before entering college; and adults who want to earn continuing education credits, certificates, or degrees through distance education. The 1989 edition listed courses from seventy-one colleges, but the latest edition includes over thirteen thousand courses from 140 accredited institutions. A good overview of the college credit system, transfer of credits, testing for credits, tuition and fees, sources of financial aid, and advice for potential students.

You can find colleges by geographic area or find a course by subject area and grade level, from elementary to graduate study. Some courses include audio or video cassettes, computer-aided instruction, or lab kits.

Ravitch, D. *The Language Police: How Pressure Groups Restrict What Students Learn* (Knopf, 2003).

An education historian, Ravitch was a member of the National Assessment Governing Board, a nonpartisan national testing review board. But according to Ravitch, some test publishers aren't satisfied with the board's review—they appoint their own committees and boards to delete questionable or objectionable test materials. An excerpt from the chapter, "Forbidden Topics, Forbidden Words" appeared in the Fall 2003 *Authors Guild Bulletin*. After reading Ravitch's account of the ridiculous reasons that the so-called bias and sensitivity committee of a major publisher of standardized tests recommended deleting words, phrases, and ideas from an elementary-level reading test, I didn't know whether to scream or cry. One of the most ludicrous examples of sensitivity screening involved a true story about a blind man who hiked to the top of Mount McKinley. The committee voted almost unanimously to delete the story because it took place in the mountains (children who do not live near mountains might feel excluded) and because the story described the man as blind (blindness might imply a disadvantage, and a blind person might be insulted by being admired for achieving a difficult task). In Ravitch's words: "Some of this censorship is trivial, some is ludicrous, and some of it is breathtaking in its power to dumb down what children learn in school."

Steinem, G. *Revolution from Within: A Book of Self-Esteem* (Little, Brown, 1992).

Although this book is subtitled *A Book of Self-Esteem*, much of it has to do with learning, testing, and educational systems.

Three sections of this book provide a lot of interesting, informative, and sometimes surprising information: "The Importance of Un-Learning," "Re-Learning," and "Bodies of Knowledge." Before reading this book, for example, I was unaware of the nineteenth-century popularity of a science called craniology, whereby the size of a person's skull supposedly indicated the level of his or her intelligence, and I did not know that the IQ tests so commonly used in schools were originally designed by Alfred Binet to identify learning-disabled young children simply in order to help them. When the tests reached the United States, they were mass-produced and used to exclude people or categorize them.

On the question of competition, Steinem summarizes the research of psychologist Alfie Kohn, who concludes that "superior performance not only does not require competition; it usually seems to require its absence" (page 189). She also presents the results of a research study seeking the reason for Asian American students' disproportionately high achievement in math and science; researchers concluded that the students succeeded because they studied in groups and helped each other. Yet our schools continue to pit students against each other for grades.

With footnotes and multiple references to scholarly abstracts and studies, this is not a quick and easy read. But the knowledge Steinem presents is worth the effort.

Abstracts, Articles, and Research

Bouldoukian, J., Wilkins, A. J., & Evans, B.J.W. (2002). Randomised controlled trial of the effect of coloured overlays
on the rate of reading of people with specific learning difficulties. *Ophthalmic and Physiological Optics, 22,* 55–60.

For those who need scientific proof that scotopic sensitivity
exists and that colored transparent overlays can alleviate many
reading problems, here's the proof. This is one of the most stringent
studies and, of course, includes references to related studies and
topics.

Cohen, R. "Schoolhouse Rot." *Mother Jones,* Jan. 10, 2001.
http://www.motherjones.com/news/feature/2001/01/soda.html.

This article discusses the alarming practice of schools accepting
multimillion dollar contracts for exclusive rights to market sodas on
their campuses. (One of the most notorious cases involved a 1997
fiasco in which Coca-Cola promised $8 million to a school in Col-
orado Springs over a ten-year period, as long as the students drank
seventy thousand cases of Coke products for the first three years of
the contract.) The article also references studies that link soda consumption to osteoporosis, diabetes, and obesity among children.

Few people were aware that when laws in 1999 required
schools to stop selling sodas during meal times, some soda manufacturers started giving kids free sodas. Parents need to find out
what foods and beverages are being marketed to their children and
support school administrators who take a stand on behalf of children's health.

http://www.homeschool.com

This is a good place for parents to start their search for information and support on homeschooling. Although many of the
links lead to advertisements for products, online courses, and professional services, there is enough free information to merit a visit
to this site, including an online newsletter.

A click on the Approaches link will provide a basic overview of different teaching methods, including Montessori, Waldorf, and Unschooling. After reading the summary, parents will have some ideas about methods that might work best for their own children and will have a starting point for their research into teaching techniques and theories.

The Click Learning section provides links to Web sites that provide activities and lessons in different subject areas, such as science, reading, and math.

Resources Guide offers an array of topics from art and music to computer skills, current events, travel, and information about homeschooling in different states.

Hughes, G. "Have You Had Your Ritalin Today?"
http://www.impactpress.com/articles/decjan01/ritalin120101.html,
     December 2000.

Hughes explains how Ritalin works; quotes convincingly from the Merrow Report's investigative piece *A.D.D. A Dubious Diagnosis*, which aired on PBS; and suggests that many kids who are diagnosed as ADHD are actually gifted. Hughes is concerned that the very people who treat disorders are the same ones who officially define them.

Tansey, M. A. "Ten Year Stability of EEG Biofeedback Results
     for a 10 Year Old Hyperactive Boy Who Failed Fourth
     Grade Perceptually Impaired Class." *Biofeedback and*
     Self-Regulation, **1993,** *18,* **33–34.**
http://www.snr-jnt.org/NFBArch/Reprints/mat_10.htm.

I followed one link that involved using biofeedback training for a ten-year-old hyperactive boy with developmental reading disorder and ocular instability. The abstract reported that use of biofeedback training had alleviated all three symptoms, which had not returned during the following two years. Another link showed a ten-year follow-up study on the same boy: he had successfully completed high school and was currently enrolled in college and earning a 2.50 grade point average.

"Therapeutic Uses: ADD/ADHD." *EEG Spectrum International.*
http://www.eegspectrum.com/applications/ADHD-ADD/

I found the case studies profiled on this Web site particularly interesting because they use a multifaceted approach to treating kids diagnosed as ADD-ADHD. Among the profiles are those of a fifteen-year-old girl, two nine-year-old boys, and a thirteen-year-old boy. The thirteen-year-old boy was rebellious, defiant, and disruptive in school and occasionally suffered from bed-wetting. His parents had their own problems with alcohol and drugs, so they did not want to place the boy on medication. Instead, they took him to the Center for Educational and Personal Development (CEPD), which specialized in brainwave-based biofeedback. In addition, the CEPD staff measured the boy's brain activity and found that it had too much slow-wave activity, which made it difficult for him to learn. The CEPD treatment plan included individual counseling, nutritional changes that included eliminating caffeine and reducing sugar, guidance to help his mother learn to prepare well-balanced meals, substance abuse counseling for the mother, and neurofeedback training for the boy (which involved using specialized computer software in a video game format that enabled him to monitor and alter his brain-wave functioning). When he started, the boy could not sit still and focus for even one minute. After forty sessions his attention span had increased to approximately forty-five minutes; within six months his reading and math scores had increased by a full grade level, and he made the honor roll at his alternative school.

In addition to the individual case profiles, this Web site has a link to a list of abstracts and technical papers.

Index

A

About Discipline.com, 195

Academic achievement: by ADHD student, 153–155; and competition, 208; by special ed student, 96–98. *See also* Grades

Accountability, testing teachers for, 19–20

ADD. *See* Attention deficit disorder (ADD)

ADHD. *See* Attention deficit disorder (ADD)

Adjectives, for describing students, 91–92, 171

Administrators: classroom experience of, 26, 27; dream school facilities for, 178–181; ease of, vs. children's needs, 26, 172; humiliation modeled by, 29; reducing number of, 17–18; as substitute teachers, 54; suggestions for dealing with new teachers, 51–64; and teacher burnout, 93

African-American Unschooling Web site, 195–196

Age, students grouped by, 4, 27, 172

Amen, D. G., 203–204

American Academy of Neurology, 158–159

American Heart Association, 150

"Amnesty" technique, for motivating students, 89–90

Amphetamines, for ADD-ADHD, 156–160. *See also* Medicating students

Armstrong, T., 168–169

Aron, E., 204–205

Articles. *See* Resources

Aspartame, 144, 199–200

At-risk students: motivating, 91–92; terminology for, 91, 171

Atomoxetine, 160

Attendance: dream school's procedures on, 180–181; emphasis on, 25; and making schools desirable places to be, 29

Attention deficit disorder (ADD), 153–170; academic achievement by student with, 153–155; alternative approaches to, 160, 163–164, 167, 205, 210–211; author's unanswered questions about, 163; and giftedness, 157, 210; and nutrition, 163, 166–167, 167–168; reasons for prescribing drugs for, 161–162; resources on, 165–170, 196–197, 202, 203–204, 205, 210–211; and sleep deprivation, 168. *See also* Medicating students

Attention deficit hyperactivity disorder (ADHD). *See* Attention deficit disorder (ADD)

B

Behavior, reasons for, 46–50, 80, 98

Behavior disordered (BD) label, 103–107

Behavior problems: due to inattention to reason for child's behavior, 98–103; feelings as root of, 112–113; and journal writing, 46–50, 112; by students with reading problems, 74–75, 89–90, 139. *See also* Tardiness

Berne, S. A., 205

Binet, A., 208

Biofeedback, resources on, 163–164, 210, 211

Black children, skin color as issue for, 118–119

Block, M, A., 169
Body language: of students, 78; of teacher, 52, 70
Books. *See* Resources
Bordessa, K., 196
Bouldoukian, J., 140, 209
Boyce, W. T., 174
Brain Connection Web site, 197–198
Brain function: and essential fatty acids (EFAs), 144–145, 146–148; and high-fructose corn syrup, 144, 145–146; of misbehaving children, 10–11; Web site on, 197–198
Breast milk, and infant brain activity, 146
Breggin, P. R., 170
Bullying: children's response to, 114–115; in dream school, 182
Bus drivers, 84

C

Carbo, M., 134, 141, 201
Center for Educational and Personal Development (CEPD), 211
Child development, individual variation in rates of, 27, 94, 116
Children and Adults with Attention Deficit Disorder (CHADD), 158–159, 161–162, 165, 167, 197
Class periods, length of, 26
Class rosters, for new teachers, 63–64
Class size: dream school, 189; reducing, 15, 93–94; uniform, 27, 172
Classroom management: author's first success with, 39–43; and medicating ADD-ADHD students, 162; by new teachers, 51–53, 82; respect-based approach to, 76–80; taught in teacher training, 82. *See also* Behavior problems; Detention; Discipline
Classrooms: administrators visiting, of new teachers, 58–59; age grouping of students in, 4, 27, 172; lighting in, 182, 199; politicians in, 16, 25
Cohen, R., 209
Common sense, and problems in public schools, 18–19
Competition: and academic performance, 208. *See also* Grades
Conflict resolution process, dream school, 177, 179–180
Court-ordered living arrangements, 120–121

D

Day care, 28, 178
Detention: high cost of, 75; negative consequences of, 72–74; for tardiness, 65–66, 67, 71–72
Diller, L., 160
Discipline, 195, 198. *See also* Behavior problems; Classroom management
Discipline Without Stress, Punishments or Rewards (Marshall), 195
Disenchanted students, 91–92, 171
Divorced parents: children's feelings about, 117–118; child's fantasy about, 47–48
Drazen, J. M., 198
Dream school. *See* Totally Cool School (TCS)
Drugs, 48–50. *See also* Medicating students
Dunn, K., 200
Dunn, R., 200
Durham trial, 143, 146–148, 149
Dyslexia, 44, 140, 150, 167

E

Eberstadt, M., 166
EGG Spectrum International, 163–164
Elected officials: with children in private schools, 26; children of, in public schools, 17; in classrooms, 16; reading to children, 25
Emotions. *See* Feelings
Essential fatty acids (EFAs), 144–145, 146–151
Evans, B.J.W., 140, 209
Extracurricular activities: at dream school, 189–191; new teachers assigned to, 54–55
Eye contact: with misbehaving students, 41, 77–78, 79; to prevent behavior problems, 52

F

Fable, about American public school system, 1–14
Fat, essential fatty acids (EFAs), 144–145, 146–151
FDA, approval of aspartame, 199–200
Feelings: about bullies, 114–115; about court-ordered living arrangements, 120–121; about divorced parents, 47–48, 117–118; about friendships, 115–116, 122–123; about parents belittling children, 116, 121–122;

about relevance of school learning, 126–128; about skin color, 118–120; about teachers picking on students, 123–126; author's childhood, 113; journal writing to deal with, 111–112; role of, in learning, 174; as root of behavior problems, 112–113

Feingold diet, 167–168

Fielding, R., 199

Financial perks, for new teachers, 61–62

Fitness program, dream school, 187–188

Food. *See* Nutrition

Foreign languages: author's experience with, 37; in dream school, 183–184; and teacher training, 21

Formula, and infant brain activity, 146

Freed, J., 165–166

Friends: being your own, 119; demanding exclusivity, 122–123; losing/attracting, 115–116

G

Gallagher, T., 165, 197

Gangs, 50

Gap between rich and poor, 3–4, 17

Grades: of ADHD student, 153–155; for children learning to read, 25–26; and detention for tardiness, 66; electronic system for, 59–60; lessened requirements for, 5, 6; nonimportance of, 92; parent belittling child for, 116; and possibility of success, 42–43; of special ed student, 96–97. *See also* Academic achievement

Grammar, in journals, 44

Greene, A., 168

Greene, T., 149

Growth hormones, 160

Guardians. *See* Parents/guardians

H

Handwriting, 44

Hartmann, T., 169

"Have You Had Your Ritalin Today?" (Hughes), 157, 210

Hayes, A., 199–200

Healing ADD (Amen), 203–204

High school diploma, financial benefit of, 127

High-fructose corn syrup, 144, 145–146

The Highly Sensitive Person (Aron), 204–205

Holt, J. C., 206

Home Education Resource Guide (Hubbs), 206

Homeschooling: Africentric, 195–196; considerations before beginning, 85; resources on, 85–86, 195–196, 206–207, 209–210

How Children Fail (Holt), 206

How Children Learn (Holt), 206

How to Get Fat Without Really Trying (ABC News), 150–151

Hubbs, D., 206

Hughes, G., 157, 210

I

Ideal school. *See* Totally Cool School (TCS)

Illiteracy, of prison inmates, 75–76

In-school suspension (ISS) programs, 72–73. *See also* Detention

Independent Study Catalog, 207

"Institutions, Contracts, and Academic Freedom" (Drazen), 198–199

Irlen, H., 134

Irlen Institute, 136, 140

J

Jennings, P., 150–151

Johnson, L.: acting experience of, 35–36; childhood feelings of, 113; first teaching position of, 38–43; foreign language experience of, 37; navy career of, 36–38; questions on ADD, 163; undergraduate college experience of, 33–35, 36, 37

Johnston, L., 199–200

Journal writing, 43–50; anonymity in, 44, 45, 46; content-only grading of, 44; on design for new school, 172; handwriting in, 44; preceding independent reading, 111–112; reasons for behaviors revealed in, 46–50; topics for, 45

Juvenile offenders, with reading problems, 76

K

Kohn, A., 208

L

Labels, educational, 95–110; applied to young misbehaving student, 98–103; behavior disordered (BD), 103–107;

examples of students with, 107–109; parents' belief in, 96–98; prevalence of, 95–96; questions about, 30; school funding linked to, 95, 161; suggested new, 110

Language, foul, 30

The Language Police (Ravitch), 207–208

Lawsuits: against school systems, 27–28, 29; threat of, 108

Learning, role of feelings in, 174

Learning All the Time (Holt), 206

Learning disabilities: labeling students with, 96–98; and nutrition, 145, 147–148; testing students with, 109

Learning styles, 29

Learning Styles Network, 200

Lesson plans: difficulty of creating, 16; dream school, 184–185; for new teachers, 60–61; Web site offering, 203

Letters: from children, 114–128; from teachers and parents, 82–94; thanking teachers, 193–194

The Light Barrier (Stone), 134

Lighting: computers and television, 204; dream school, 182; resource on, 199. *See also* Scotopic sensitivity

"Lighting the Learning Environment" (Fielding), 199

Literacy rates: of prison inmates, 75–76; of students throughout world, 7–8

M

Madden, C., 135

Marshall, M., 195

Maturation, variation in rates of, 27, 94, 116–117

McCauley Family Learning Center, 141

Medicating Kids (PBS Frontline), 167

Medicating students, 10–11, 153–170; alternatives to, 160, 163–164, 205; common-sense test applied to, 18–19; controversy over, 156–160, 202; future of, 163–164; questions about, 29–30; reasons for, 161–162; resources on, 165–170, 205, 210

Mentors, for new teachers, 57–58

Methylphenidate. *See* Ritalin

Money. *See* School funding

Motivating students: "amnesty" technique for, 89–90; electronic grading for, 60; who have given up on school, 91–92

Multiculturalism, teaching, 86–87

N

National Reading Styles Institute (NRSI), 134, 136, 141, 201

Neurobiological disorders, and nutrition, 145, 147–148

New England Journal of Medicine, 198–199

New teachers, 51–64; class rosters for, 63–64; classroom management by, 51–53, 82; electronic grading by, 59–60; extracurricular assignments for, 54–55; financial perks for, 61–62; lesson plans for, 60–61; nutrition for, 62; phones/intercoms for, 58; portfolio design taught to, 62–63; professional development of, 53–54, 55, 57–58; supporting, 56–57, 58–59; teaching load for, 53, 61–62; thanking, 64. *See also* Teachers

Null, G., 165

Nutrition, 143–151; aspartame, 199–200; and attention deficit disorder (ADD), 163, 166–167, 167–168; dream school, 175–176; Durham trial, 143, 146–148, 149; essential fatty acids (EFAs), 144–145, 146–151; high-fructose corn syrup, 144, 145–146; and neurobiological disorders, 145, 147–148; for new teachers, 62; resources on, 149–151; soft drinks, 8, 25, 209

P

Parents/guardians: children belittled by, 116–117, 121–122; and court-ordered living arrangements, 120–121; divorced, 47–48, 117–118; label's effect on, 96–98; meeting with, 84–85; reasons for noncooperation by, 83–84; telephoning, 58; and testing, 84–85; thanking, of well-behaved students, 77

Parsons, L., 165–166

Pharmaceutical companies: and aspartame, 199–200; and medicating children, 10–11, 161; pro-Ritalin video funded by, 161–162, 167; and research on drugs, 198

Pharmacracy, 202

Phones, for new teachers, 58

Piedmont Community Charter School (Gastonia, NC), 135

Piercings, 27

Politicians. *See* Elected officials

Portfolios, teaching new teachers about, 62–63

Portwood, M., 143, 145, 146, 147
Positive affirmations, 121
Prejudices, 86–87
Preschool, 28
Prison: illiteracy of inmates, 75–76; seen as best option, 48
Public school professors, 21
Public schools: assumptions underlying, 172; children of elected officials in, 17; common sense applied to, 18–19; elected officials in, 16, 25; fable about, 1–14; hours of, 28; lawsuits against, 27–28, 29; questions about, 25–31; size of, 4, 8, 13, 30. *See also* School funding; Totally Cool School (TCS)
Punishment, effect on behavior in long term, 172

Q

Queen of education: edicts of, 15–23; questions posed by, 25–31
Queen's common-sense test (QCST), 18–19
Questions: about ADD, 163; about public schools, 25–31

R

"Randomised controlled trial of the effect of coloured overlays" (Bouldakian, Wilkins, and Evans), 140, 209
Ravitch, D., 207–208
Reading: at dream school, 187; independent, journal writing preceding, 111–112; out loud, 42, 91; teaching, 25–26, 196, 201–202
Reading & Writing Consultants Inc., 141
"Reading and Perpetual Motion" (Bordessa), 196
Reading by the Colors (Irlen), 134
Reading Lady.com, 201–202
Reading problems: helping students overcome, 90–91; misbehavior by students with, 74–75, 89–90, 139; prison inmates and juvenile offenders with, 75–76. *See also* Scotopic sensitivity
Resources, 195–211; attention deficit disorder (ADD), 160, 165–170, 196–197, 202, 203–204, 205, 210–211; biofeedback, 163–164, 210–211, 211; discipline, 195, 198; essential fatty acids (EFAs), 149–151; homeschooling, 85–86, 195–196, 206–207, 209–210; medicating children, 165–170, 205,

210; nutrition, 149–151; scotopic sensitivity, 134, 140–141, 201, 209; teaching reading, 196, 201–202
Respect: classroom management based on, 52, 76–80; expected of children, 28; multiculturalism taught through, 86–87
Restrooms: dream school, 183; inadequate facilities in, 25; rules on use of, 27; tardiness due to inaccessibility of, 69–71
Revolution from Within (Steinem), 208
Right-Brained Children in a Left-Brained World (Freed and Parsons), 165–166
Ritalin: alternatives to, 160, 163–164, 205; CHADD video on, 161–162, 167; controversy over use of, 156–160, 202; questions about use of, 29; reasons for widespread use of, 161–162; resources on, 166, 170, 210. *See also* Medicating students
Rotella, P., 150

S

Salaries: of new teachers, 61–62; of teachers, 27, 30–31
School boards, 27
School buildings: dream school, 172–173, 181, 182–183, 188–189; questions about, 28–29, 30, 31
School funding: educational labels linked to, 95, 161; inadequacy of, 8, 31; in poor neighborhoods, 3–4; priorities in allocating, 19, 28; test results linked to, 88; vs. money for drugs for children, 161
"Schoolhouse Rot" (Cohen), 209
Schools. *See* Public schools
Scotopic sensitivity, 129–141; current research on, 136–137; discussed with students, 90–91; experiences with students with, 129–133, 135, 138–140; increasing acceptance of idea of, 135–136; Irlen system for, 133–134; NRSI overlays for, 201; resources on, 134, 140–141, 201, 209; testing students for, 137–138
Scotopic Sensitivity Syndrome (SSS), defined, 134
Security: dream school, 173, 175, 181–182, 183; lacking in schools, 26; necessity of, 173–174; in restrooms, 70–71

Self-image, ways to improve, 119, 122
Self-respect, helping students develop, 86–87
Shepard, D. H., 132
Skin color, as reason for being picked on, 118–120
Sleep deprivation, and attention deficit disorder (ADD), 168
Soft drinks, 8, 25, 209
Sousa, D., 174
Special education, parents' belief in child's placement in, 96–98
Spelling, 44, 154–155, 206
Staff development, improving, 55
Standardized testing. *See* Testing students
Steinem, G., 208
Stone, R., 134
Strattera, 160
Student teaching, length and timing of, 83
Students: adjectives to describe, 91–92, 171; divided equally among teachers, 172; foul language use by, 30; hitting teachers, 98–103; with piercings, 27; violent, 9–10, 98–103. *See also* Medicating students; Motivating students; Testing students
Substitute teachers: administrators as, 54; invitation to become, 94
Success, students' belief in possibility of, 43
Sugar. *See* Aspartame; High-fructose corn syrup
Summer school, new teachers teaching, 61–62
"Sweetener Probed" (Johnston), 199–200
Szasz, T., 202

T

Tansey, M. A., 210–211
Tardiness: alternative procedure for handling, 65–66, 67–71; detention for, 65–66, 67, 71–72; and time between high school classes, 26
Teacher training: classroom management taught in, 82; entrance requirements for, 20, 22–23; inadequacy of, 82–83; reforming, 20–23, 83
Teachers: author's first position as, 38–43; avoiding burnout of, 92–93; difficulty of profession of, 15–16; hitting students, 104–107; humiliating students,

29; leaving profession, 82–83; new title for, 21; picking on students, 123–126; reasons for becoming, 22; salaries of, 27, 30–31; shortage if, 21, 22; students divided equally among, 172; substitute, 54, 94; testing, 19–22; and testing students, 85, 87–88; thanking, 193–194. *See also* New teachers
Teachers.Net, 203
Test anxiety, 88
Testing students, 11–12; censorship in materials for, 207–208; dream school, 184, 185–186; with learning disabilities, 109; long-term consequences of, 93; lower-level thinking as focus in, 29, 87–89; parents' frustration with, 85; school funding linked to, 88; for scotopic sensitivity, 137–138; students' dislike of school due to, 85; teachers' frustration with, 85, 87–88
Testing teachers: after licensing, 19–20; at end of training, 20, 21; for psychological fitness, 21–22
Texans for Safe Education, 164
Thanking: new teachers, 64; parents/guardians of well-behaved children, 77; students for good behavior, 77, 80; teachers, 193–194
Thinking skills, school learning to improve, 126–127
Time-outs, 52–53, 78–79
Totally Cool School (TCS), 171–191; academic program, 183–185, 186–187; administration facilities, 178–181; attendance procedures, 180–181; conflict resolution process, 177, 179–180; exterior and grounds, 172–173, 188–189; extracurricular offerings, 189–191; fitness program, 187–188; food and nutrition, 175–176; interiors, 181, 182–183; restrooms, 183; security measures, 173, 175, 181–182, 183; size of school and classes, 177–178, 189; testing, 184, 185–186

U

University of Glamorgan (South Wales), 134, 140
U.S. Drug Enforcement Administration (DEA), on medications for ADD-ADHD, 157–160

V

Violence: and labeling of students, 108–109; by students, 9–10, 98–103

W

Walton, S. C., 196
Web sites. *See* Resources
White children, skin color as issue for, 119–120
Whiting, Paul, 136–137
"Why Ritalin Rules" (Eberstadt), 166

Wilkins

Wilkins, A. J., 140, 209
Without Ritalin (Berne), 205
Woodworth, T., 158–160

Y

You Can Handle Them All discipline model, 198

Z

Zero stimulation, with misbehaving students, 78–79